Register for Free Membe

solutions@syngress.com

D0454147

Over the last few years, Syngress has published many best-selling and critically acclaimed books, including Tom Shinder's *Configuring ISA Server 2004*, Brian Caswell and Jay Beale's *Snort 2.0 Intrusion Detection*, and Angela Orebaugh and Gilbert Ramirez's *Ethereal Packet Sniffing*. One of the reasons for the success of these books has been our unique **solutions@syngress.com** program. Through this site, we've been able to provide readers a real time extension to the printed book.

As a registered owner of this book, you will qualify for free access to our members-only solutions@syngress.com program. Once you have registered, you will enjoy several benefits, including:

- Four downloadable e-booklets on topics related to the book. Each booklet is approximately 20-30 pages in Adobe PDF format. They have been selected by our editors from other best-selling Syngress books as providing topic coverage that is directly related to the coverage in this book.

- A comprehensive FAQ page that consolidates all of the key points of this book into an easy-to-search web page, providing you with the concise, easy-to-access data you need to perform your job.

- A "From the Author" Forum that allows the authors of this book to post timely updates links to related sites, or additional topic coverage that may have been requested by readers.

Just visit us at **www.syngress.com/solutions** and follow the simple registration process. You will need to have this book with you when you register.

Thank you for giving us the opportunity to serve your needs. And be sure to let us know if there is anything else we can do to make your job easier.

SYNGRESS®

SYNGRESS®

Perfect Passwords

SELECTION, PROTECTION, AUTHENTICATION

Mark Burnett

Dave Kleiman Technical Editor

Syngress Publishing, Inc., the author(s), and any person or firm involved in the writing, editing, or production (collectively "Makers") of this book ("the Work") do not guarantee or warrant the results to be obtained from the Work.

There is no guarantee of any kind, expressed or implied, regarding the Work or its contents. The Work is sold AS IS and WITHOUT WARRANTY. You may have other legal rights, which vary from state to state.

In no event will Makers be liable to you for damages, including any loss of profits, lost savings, or other incidental or consequential damages arising out from the Work or its contents. Because some states do not allow the exclusion or limitation of liability for consequential or incidental damages, the above limitation may not apply to you.

You should always use reasonable care, including backup and other appropriate precautions, when working with computers, networks, data, and files.

Syngress Media®, Syngress®, "Career Advancement Through Skill Enhancement®," "Ask the Author UPDATE®," and "Hack Proofing®," are registered trademarks of Syngress Publishing, Inc. "Syngress: The Definition of a Serious Security Library"™, "Mission Critical™," and "The Only Way to Stop a Hacker is to Think Like One™" are trademarks of Syngress Publishing, Inc. Brands and product names mentioned in this book are trademarks or service marks of their respective companies.

KEY	SERIAL NUMBER
001	HJIRTCV764
002	PO9873D5FG
003	829KM8NJH2
004	83TMSW28HT
005	CVPLQ6WQ23
006	VBP965T5T5
007	HJJJ863WD3E
008	2987GVTWMK
009	629MP5SDJT
010	IMWQ295T6T

PUBLISHED BY
Syngress Publishing, Inc.
800 Hingham Street
Rockland, MA 02370

Perfect Passwords: Selection, Protection, Authentication

Copyright © 2006 by Syngress Publishing, Inc. All rights reserved. Printed in Canada. Except as permitted under the Copyright Act of 1976, no part of this publication may be reproduced or distributed in any form or by any means, or stored in a database or retrieval system, without the prior written permission of the publisher, with the exception that the program listings may be entered, stored, and executed in a computer system, but they may not be reproduced for publication.

Printed in Canada
1 2 3 4 5 6 7 8 9 0
ISBN: 1-59749-041-5

Publisher: Andrew Williams   Page Layout and Art: Patricia Lupien
Acquisitions Editor: Gary Byrne   Copy Editors: Michael McGee, Judy Eby
Technical Editor: Dave Kleiman   Indexer: Julie Kawabata
Cover Designer: Michael Kavish

Distributed by O'Reilly Media, Inc. in the United States and Canada.

For information on rights, translations, and bulk purchases contact Matt Pedersen, Director of Sales and Rights, at Syngress Publishing; email matt@syngress.com or fax to 781-681-3585.

Acknowledgments

Syngress would like to acknowledge the following people for their kindness and support in making this book possible.

Syngress books are now distributed in the United States and Canada by O'Reilly Media, Inc. The enthusiasm and work ethic at O'Reilly are incredible, and we would like to thank everyone there for their time and efforts to bring Syngress books to market: Tim O'Reilly, Laura Baldwin, Mark Brokering, Mike Leonard, Donna Selenko, Bonnie Sheehan, Cindy Davis, Grant Kikkert, Opol Matsutaro, Steve Hazelwood, Mark Wilson, Rick Brown, Tim Hinton, Kyle Hart, Sara Winge, Peter Pardo, Leslie Crandell, Regina Aggio Wilkinson, Pascal Honscher, Preston Paull, Susan Thompson, Bruce Stewart, Laura Schmier, Sue Willing, Mark Jacobsen, Betsy Waliszewski, Kathryn Barrett, John Chodacki, Rob Bullington, Kerry Beck, Karen Montgomery, and Patrick Dirden.

The incredibly hardworking team at Elsevier Science, including Jonathan Bunkell, Ian Seager, Duncan Enright, David Burton, Rosanna Ramacciotti, Robert Fairbrother, Miguel Sanchez, Klaus Beran, Emma Wyatt, Krista Leppiko, Marcel Koppes, Judy Chappell, Radek Janousek, Rosie Moss, David Lockley, Nicola Haden, Bill Kennedy, Martina Morris, Kai Wuerfl-Davidek, Christiane Leipersberger, Yvonne Grueneklee, Nadia Balavoine, and Chris Reinders for making certain that our vision remains worldwide in scope.

David Buckland, Marie Chieng, Lucy Chong, Leslie Lim, Audrey Gan, Pang Ai Hua, Joseph Chan, June Lim, and Siti Zuraidah Ahmad of Pansing Distributors for the enthusiasm with which they receive our books.

David Scott, Tricia Wilden, Marilla Burgess, Annette Scott, Andrew Swaffer, Stephen O'Donoghue, Bec Lowe, Mark Langley, and Anyo Geddes of Woodslane for distributing our books throughout Australia, New Zealand, Papua New Guinea, Fiji, Tonga, Solomon Islands, and the Cook Islands.

Author

 **Mark Burnett** is a recognized security consultant, author, and researcher who specializes in hardening Microsoft Windows-based servers and networks. He has spent nearly a decade developing unique strategies and techniques for locking down Windows servers and maintaining his specialized expertise of Windows security. Mark is coauthor and technical editor of *Microsoft Log Parser Toolkit* (Syngress Publishing, ISBN: 1-932266-52-6), author of *Hacking the Code: ASP.NET Web Application Security* (Syngress Publishing, ISBN: 1-932266-65-8), coauthor of *Maximum Windows 2000 Security* (SAMS Publishing, ISBN: 0-672319-65-9), and coauthor of *Stealing the Network: How to Own the Box* (Syngress Publishing, ISBN: 1-931836-87-6). He also contributed to *Dr. Tom Shinder's ISA Server and Beyond: Real World Security Solutions for Microsoft Enterprise Networks* (Syngress Publishing, ISBN: 1-931836-66-3) and was a contributor and technical editor for *Special Ops: Host and Network Security for Microsoft, UNIX, and Oracle* (Syngress Publishing, ISBN: 1-931836-69-8). Mark speaks at security conferences and has published dozens of security articles that have appeared in publications such as *Windows IT Pro Magazine* (formerly *Windows &.NET Magazine*), *Redmond Magazine, Windows Web Solutions, Security Administrator, SecurityFocus.com, TheRegister.co.uk,* and *WindowsSecrets.com,* among others. Microsoft has twice recognized Mark's contribution to the Windows community with the Windows Server Most Valued Professional (MVP) award.

Technical Editor

Dave Kleiman (CAS, CCE, CIFI, CISM, CISSP, ISSAP, ISSMP, MCSE) has worked in the Information Technology Security sector since 1990. Currently, he is the owner of SecurityBreachResponse.com and is the Chief Information Security Officer for Securit-e-Doc, Inc. Before starting this position, he was Vice President of Technical Operations at Intelliswitch, Inc., where he supervised an international telecommunications and Internet service provider network. Dave is a recognized security expert; a former Florida Certified Law Enforcement Officer, he specializes in computer forensic investigations, incident response, intrusion analysis, security audits, and secure network infrastructures. He has written several secure installation and configuration guides about Microsoft technologies that are used by network professionals. He has developed a Windows Operating System lockdown tool, S-Lok (www.s-doc.com/products/slok.asp), which surpasses NSA, NIST, and Microsoft Common Criteria Guidelines. Dave was a contributing author to *Microsoft Log Parser Toolkit* (Syngress Publishing, ISBN: 1-932266-52-6). He is frequently a speaker at many national security conferences and is a regular contributor to many security-related newsletters, Web sites, and Internet forums. Dave is a member of several organizations, including the International Association of Counter Terrorism and Security Professionals (IACSP), International Society of Forensic Computer Examiners® (ISFCE), Information Systems Audit and Control Association® (ISACA), High Technology Crime Investigation Association (HTCIA), Network and Systems Professionals Association (NaSPA), Association of Certified Fraud Examiners (ACFE), Anti Terrorism Accreditation

Board (ATAB), and ASIS International®. He is also a Secure Member and Sector Chief for Information Technology at The FBI's InfraGard® and a Member and Director of Education at the International Information Systems Forensics Association (IISFA).

Techical Reviewer

Ryan Russell (Blue Boar) has worked in the IT field for more than 13 years, focusing on information security for the last seven. He was the lead author of *Hack Proofing Your Network, Second Edition* (Syngress, ISBN: 1-928994-70-9), contributing author and technical editor of *Stealing the Network: How to Own the Box* (Syngress, ISBN: 1-931836-87-6) and other books in the Stealing the Network series, and a frequent technical editor for the Hack Proofing series of books from Syngress. He also was a technical adviser on *Snort 2.0 Intrusion Detection* (Syngress, ISBN: 1-931836-74-4). Ryan founded the vuln-dev mailing list and moderated it for three years under the alias "Blue Boar."

Contents

Chapter 1

Passwords: The Basics and Beyond

Solutions in this chapter:

- **The Beginning**

> ...alighting from his beast, he tied it up to a tree, and
> going to the entrance, pronounced the words which he
> had not forgotten, *"Open, Sesame!?* Hereat, as was its
> wont, the door flew open, and entering thereby he saw the
> goods and hoard of gold and silver untouched and lying as
> he had left them.

— Arabian Nights, The Forty Thieves

The Beginning

My fascination with security began perhaps a decade ago when I took my first job with the official title of software developer. I had written code casually for years, but this was the first time someone paid me to do it. I was a corporate employee. I wrote code all day. I had a network account that I logged in to every morning. Like almost everyone else at the company, I had a weak password that I swapped every three months with another weak password.

I had been interested in various aspects of security for a long time, but information at that time was scarce. Back then, you couldn't just search on Google for something; you found the good information by navigating an endless pathway of hyperlinks from one Web site to the next. The information that I did find was often obsolete, unreliable, or limited in context; thus, I was left unsatisfied.

Nevertheless, I studied everything I could find during any spare minute I had. After I read and reread stacks of printouts, they slowly started to make sense to me. Although I was merely a beginner, I learned a few tricks that enabled me to gain already some rank as the office hacker.

Then one morning I got my calling. A friend of mine who was one of the company executives pulled me into his office, explained a predicament the company faced, and told me that the company needed my help. The senior network administrator had been in a heated argument with the company vice president earlier that morning. In the middle of the argument, the network administrator slammed his keys on the table, cleared out his desk, and left the company. Now, the company management wanted me to break in to all the systems and recover all the administrator's passwords because the VP was too scorned to call the admin asking for the passwords. I knew that I didn't have the experience to take on such a task, but still I couldn't help being seduced by the challenge. I told him I would do it.

But once I sat down at my desk, reality set in; I was enormously intimidated by this undertaking. Sure, I knew a few tricks, but presuming that I could actually accomplish this task was absurd. I thought that perhaps I should have admitted to my friend that I wasn't as skilled as he thought. Had I gone too far? Had my own hubris clouded my judgment? As inconsequential as this incident might sound, it was my defining moment.

I could have failed. I would have failed that day if I had not discovered this remarkable truth about hackers: their superhuman skills don't make them successful; rather, everyone else fails so much at security that hackers just make it look easy. I discovered that people don't have strong passwords. Moreover, we use the same passwords repeatedly, never straying far from a few core passwords. When it comes to passwords, we just aren't that clever.

I obtained the administrator's Microsoft Access password and then his e-mail password. Next, I got his Windows NT administrator password. One password at a time his security fell—*superman12*, *superman23*, *superman95*, *Wonderwoman*.

I didn't do anything special that day except discover this decisive weakness of human security—that is, that humans are horribly predictable. Late that night I e-mailed the list of passwords to my friend. I went home, buzzing from the thrill of what I had just accomplished.

The next morning I just happened to approach the office building at the same time as the company president and vice president. They both turned, and as if they had rehearsed it beforehand, opened the front door and bowed before me. I was confused at first, but then realized that they had already heard about the passwords I had collected. I walked through the doorway feeling happy for the recognition from the top of the company. I loved the attention, but from that point on, I was infatuated—almost obsessed—with security, passwords, and the character of human behavior.

Our Passwords

Passwords, in some form or another, have long been associated with security. We see it in literature all the time: to unlock a door, to pass a guard, or to distinguish friend from enemy. These ambiguous words or phrases are the keys to magical spells or the secret codes to identify one spy to another.

Secret codes are an indispensable part of our modern lives. We use them to check our e-mail and voice mailboxes. We need them to withdraw money from an ATM or to connect to our online banking account. We use them to authorize financial transactions and to buy and sell items on the Internet. We use them to limit access to wireless Internet connections and to encrypt our most sensitive private data. You may even find yourself needing a password to order pizza, purchase flowers, rent a DVD, or get a car wash. We are a world of secrets.

Whether they are referred to as passwords, PINs, passcodes, or some other name, they are all secret keys that we hold to gain access to the protected portions of our lives.

Passwords are more than just a key. They serve several purposes. They *authenticate* us to a machine to prove our identity—a secret that only we should know. They ensure our *privacy*, keeping our sensitive information secure. They also enforce *nonrepudiation*, preventing us from later rejecting the validity of transactions authenticated with our passwords. Our username identifies us; the password validates us.

But passwords have some weaknesses: more than one person can possess knowledge of the secret at any one time. Unlike a physical key that only one person can hold at a time, you have no guarantee that someone else hasn't somehow obtained your password, with or without your knowledge. Moreover, there is a constant threat of losing your password to someone else with malicious intent. Password thefts can and do happen on a daily basis—by the thousands. Your only defense is to build a strong password, protect it carefully, and change it regularly.

The other weakness with passwords is human behavior. Human nature is such that we do not fear threats that we do not perceive. We cannot imagine why someone would want to gain access to our e-mail or network accounts. We feel reasonably safe with the passwords that we select.

That one day at work, I walked past the company president and vice president, passed through the entrance, walked down the hall, and sat down at my desk. I logged in to my network account with my own weak password and was suddenly struck with the knowledge of my own weakness. I realized that my own security was just as fragile as the security system that I had broken the day before. Just seeing my last two passwords, someone could easily guess my current password and probably the next one after that. At least one other coworker already knew my password because I shared it with him one day when I was out sick so that he could access my files. I decided that day to change my attitude about passwords.

Silly Human Behavior

A number of years ago, I sat in an audience and watched a performance of the amazing Kreskin, a self-proclaimed mentalist. I watched as he consistently predicted and manipulated the human behavior of the audience. During his tricks, he explained that he didn't have any special powers, just an extraordinary understanding of human behavior.

He consistently guessed secrets selected by the audience and related facts about the personal lives of many audience members, facts such as their social security numbers or dates of birth. He is not alone. Psychics, fortune-tellers, mediums, magicians, and others often depend on human predictability for the success of their crafts. Undoubtedly, people just behave the same.

If you ask someone to name a vegetable, 98 percent of the time, that person will tell you a carrot. Tell someone to pick an even number between 50 and 100, where both digits are different, most commonly people will pick the number 68. Think of a card. The most common choices predictably are nine of diamonds, ace of spades, queen of hearts, or the six of clubs.

You might even find yourself with exceptional skills at predicting human nature, anticipating the behavior of others, for example, or guessing the ends of movies. Remarkably, as poor as we are at avoiding predictability, we are exceptionally capable of detecting predictability in others.

Consider the list of random passwords shown in Table 1.1. If you study the list for a few minutes, you will start to see simple and predictable patterns emerge.

Table 1.1 Random Passwords

bmw66	fuzzy1	trisha
Jessica1	Steven	123456
sa1856	Alexis	gregory2
843520	xmen94	brutus1
0214866	link11	lakers7
m9153p	1nani1	lamacod1
cyril87	Bubba1	pariz2
7082382	856899	letmein
100265	grady6	tiger69
jimmyd2	mpick1	cats999
wes333	mjordan2	supra1
053092	sti2000	bearcub
4Obelix	usa123	wargame6
6Bueler	Lieve27	dan1028
Franc1	3089172	13crow
Nicole3	Roswell	ncc1701
elin97	67bird	jun0214
toyota4	rat22	password

The amazing thing is that this small list accurately represents the nature of human passwords. I could give you a list of a thousand or even a million passwords, and you would learn little more about passwords than you could from this small list.

I know because I have actually done it. Over the years I have collected real passwords from every source I could find. I have collected almost 4 million passwords, and my list continues to grow through an automated set of tools that scour the Internet for passwords, often using nothing more than ordinary search engines such as Google. I collected these passwords to gain a better understanding of how people select passwords. For five years I collected, researched, and stared at passwords—thousands of *QWERTY*s, thousands of *12345*s.

The most amazing discovery I made was absolutely nothing. Having more passwords did not change any of my password statistics; the choices of characters remained the same. The top 500 passwords were mostly the same. Password length, complexity, and lack of creativity—all unchanged.

In fact, my numbers were pretty close to other password studies conducted decades ago. Passwords were—and still are—predictably the same over and over: a number or two at the end, a couple of numbers at the beginning, all numbers, names of loved ones, dates, vehicles, sports teams, pop culture references, and the ever-present *letmein* and *password*. I could collect another four million passwords and would probably get the same results.

You're Not That Clever

If anything frustrates me about passwords, it is that so many people think they are being clever or unique, but they just aren't. If you could see a million passwords, you would probably be surprised to find that your password looks a lot like everyone else's. If you have ever gone on a long flight across the continental United States, you might have noticed that there is not a lot to see but thousands of square miles of empty space. Occasionally, you pass over a cluster of civilization, but then it's right back to empty land.

That is very much what I see when I look at passwords. So many possibilities remain untouched, while thousands cluster around the same few passwords.

Over the years, I began to categorize passwords by their patterns. Here are some of the most common categories of password-writing patterns. These are examples of what you should *not* do; never follow these patterns.

Weak Wordlist Words

This category includes dictionary words, your first or last name, a common password, or a simple phrase that you are likely to find on some wordlist somewhere. These passwords are the worst because they are so vulnerable to dictionary attacks as explained in the next chapter.

- cupcake
- auto
- badger
- letmein
- Jonathon
- Red Sox
- dirty dog

Weak Wordlist Words with Numbers

Only trivially stronger than a simple wordlist word, these passwords include numbers that people add to the front or end of a password in attempt at security or to meet specific policy requirements. Here are some examples:

- deer2000
- atlanta33
- dana55
- fred1234
- 99skip

Weak Wordlist Words with Simple Obfuscation

Again, these passwords are only slightly stronger than a simple wordlist word. These passwords usually have some simple character replacements or deliberate misspellings. Here are a few examples:

- B0ngh
- g0ldf1sh
- j@ke

License Plate Passwords

These passwords include some short phrase that makes use of abbreviations, numbers, or other techniques. These passwords certainly are stronger than a wordlist word, but they are by no means unique. They often read like license plates. Here are some examples:

- sk8ordie
- just4fun
- dabomb
- kissme
- laterpeeps

Weak Wordlist Words Doubled

Most password-cracking tools will check for this simple pattern. Here are some examples:

- crabcrab
- patpat
- joejoe

Garbled Randomness

These passwords are technically more secure because they are random and less predictable, but as you will read in this book, having a password that is easy to remember and easy to type is also essential for security. Here are some examples:

- 9uxg$t5C
- Bn2#sz63j
- &fM3tc8b

Patterns or Sequences

These passwords could fall into the category of wordlist words because they are so common. These passwords include some pattern or sequence that is based on the appearance or shape of letters or on the location of the keys on the keyboard.

- QWERTY
- 123456
- xcvb
- abc123
- typewriter (all letters on the same keyboard row)

Summary

The single most important aspect of information security is strong passwords. Likewise, the single greatest security failure is weak passwords. Network administrators blame users for selecting such poor passwords, and users blame network administrators for the inconvenience of their draconian password policies.

Further complicating the problem are hundreds of thousands of software and hardware products that have been and continue to be sold with default passwords that users never get around to changing (see defaultpassword.com to understand how big this problem really is).

People select poor passwords and do little to protect them. They share their passwords with others and use the same passwords repeatedly on multiple systems. At the same time, computing power has increased along with the number and quality of tools available to hackers.

Consequently, many have predicted that passwords, at least by themselves, will someday become obsolete. I hear people talk about retina or fingerprint scanners, but at some point, security will still involve some secret, some password.

The good news is that passwords don't have to be obsolete. In this book, I describe techniques for how you can build very strong passwords and explain how to protect your password from attack. All we need to do is follow some simple rules, use some basic common sense, and treat our passwords like real secrets. By implementing these practices, we can extend the life of this simple method of authentication.

The age of the password is not over yet.

Chapter 2

Meet Your Opponent

Solutions in this chapter:

- The Cracker
- Password Cracking

The Cracker

Password cracking is the method of employing various techniques and tools to guess, methodically determine, or otherwise obtain a password to gain unauthorized access to a protected resource. Password cracking is sometimes used to legitimately recover a lost password, and sometimes an administrator will use password cracking to test user passwords. But, for the most part, password cracking is used to steal passwords.

Some call it a game; others, a crime. But whatever it is called, both the most talented computer professionals and the novice use it. As one hacker told me, "[Password cracking] is power… the power to compel a system to yield its knowledge."

I met that hacker in an IRC room. Well known in the hacking underground for his specialized password-cracking software, this hacker agreed to speak with me on conditions of anonymity—not even a reference to his pseudonym. "I'm not a hacker or an exploiter. I just crack passwords," he told me, "but still everyone calls me a hacker. Hacker, cracker; it's all the same."

Why does he do it? "For trading, selling, sharing," he told me. "It gets me respect, and, hey, it's fun and addicting," he explained, "and I'm not the only one doing this; it goes on all the time."

This is the reality. There are people who steal passwords for some form of gain, and it happens all the time.

Why *My* Password?

Perhaps the most common question I hear when it comes to security is, why would one individual have anything tantalizing enough for a hacker to steal his or her passwords? One reason for hackers' attacks might be to disguise their identities for purposes such as sending spam, or the attack might be just one jump in the process of leapfrogging toward bigger targets. The attack might be to perform financial transactions to defraud others, or it might be to gain access to one of your subscribed services. The fact is that you cannot even comprehend the ways in which your password would be useful to another.

Password theft is a huge problem. Some Web sites are obviously more attractive targets, but no target, no matter how small, is exempt from this problem.

Password Cracking

Password cracking, once a specialized skill, is now available to just about anyone using widely available tools with names like L0phtcrack, John the Ripper, and Cain & Abel. However, before learning about password-cracking techniques, it is important to understand how a system stores your password.

Plaintext, Encryption, and Hashes

A system can use three basic methods to store your password. Every time you enter your password, the system must have some method to determine if you entered the correct password. It must store *something*.

The first—and most obvious—method is simply storing your password exactly as you entered it. This *plaintext* method stores the plain data without any obfuscation, encryption, or encoding. When you log in to your computer or a network account, it can compare the password entered with the copy stored in a database. If they match, it lets you in. The problem with this method is that you cannot always trust the security of the database. Certain users on the system will have privileges to view these databases, and therefore, all passwords would be in plain view. This method also carries a huge risk because if a hacker gains access to the database, that hacker instantly has everyone's passwords.

Imagine how hotels provided you with room keys before the days of magnetic cards. The front desk clerk would turn around to a large board representing all the rooms in the hotel, pull a key off a hook, and hand it to you. However, a couple of spare keys to your room would still be on the hook. In other words, anyone who could walk behind the hotel desk could obtain the key to your hotel room. This is approximately equivalent to storing passwords in plain text. They are available to anyone within arm's reach.

Although the plaintext method provides little password security, far too many applications still use it to protect sensitive passwords. Many software developers still have limited security training, and they repeatedly make the mistake of relying on the plaintext method.

Another method is to *encrypt* each password before storing it in the database. Encryption combines plain text with another secret key to create a garbled string that can be retrieved only by using that same key. In other words, encryption is just storing a password protected by a password. Again, anyone with that master password would have access to the entire database, making it only a little more secure than plaintext.

Using the previous example of hotel keys, encryption would be equivalent to having all hotel keys in a locked box, and only front desk employees had a copy of the master key. This method is somewhat more secure, if you trust those employees.

Password encryption is generally not acceptable for many purposes, but it certainly is better than plaintext. Sometimes, an application must store a password and retrieve the plain text for later use, and there is no way around that. For example, Windows encrypts and stores various passwords to be able to start system services and to connect to various resources. You often see this when a login dialog box pops up, and your password is already entered, represented by a string of asterisks.

TIP

When you lose your password and must retrieve it, you can tell whether a system has stored your password as plain text or if it has been encrypted. If you go through the retrieval process and the system tells you your original password, you know your password is stored in a manner that someone else could retrieve. If that's the case, your password is only as secure as the entire system's security and only as trustworthy as those managing the system.

Unfortunately, encryption also suffers when programmers lack proper security training. All too often programmers try inventing their own encryption methods or use methods that have long been proven insufficient rather than relying on time-tested, widely accepted secure encryption algorithms.

The widely accepted solution for storing passwords is to use a password hash. A hash is the result of an algorithm—a complex formula—that modifies plain text in a complicated manner to produce a garbled string that represents the password. Hashing algorithms are one-way formulas because there is no reasonable way to calculate the original password from its hash. You can't just reverse the formula.

To check your password, a system will take your entry, run it through the same hashing algorithm, and then compare the result with the data stored in the hash database. If they match, the system knows that the two passwords must have been the same to produce the same hash.

Suppose you rent a safe deposit box at a local bank. You store your most sensitive items in the box, and the bank provides you with a set of two keys (see Figure 2.1). The important thing to remember is that those are the only two keys for your box. If you lose both of those keys, the bank will have to hire a locksmith to drill out the lock to gain access to your box. If you lose your key, and the bank manager tells you that the bank can provide another copy, watch out because the bank has a spare copy somewhere.

Figure 2.1 Keys and Locks

A password hash is similar to a lock. Someone cannot easily use the lock itself to construct a new key. Therefore, you can feel quite safe that someone can possess the lock without putting your key at risk. If a system uses password hashes, you can feel reasonably safe that your password is not directly exposed. It is not completely safe (this method carries some risks that I will explain later in this chapter), but it is the safest method commonly in use.

How Your Password Falls

The method used to steal your password depends on the target system. Some passwords, such as operating system passwords, have mechanisms to lock out after several failed attempts. You might also see this with sensitive online accounts such as on banking Web sites. Other times, a hacker might be able to use techniques to launch sophisticated offline attacks that are limited only by the attacker's CPU power and patience.

The difference between an online and an offline attack is that an online attack has the protection of the system where the password is stored. Offline attacks have no protection.

Online attacks use the normal login mechanisms of a system. Faced with a login prompt, an attacker can either manually enter passwords or use some software tool to automate the process. Online attacks are normally easy to detect—and block if necessary—so they are not usually successful. With an online attack, the attacker will want to guess your password with just a few guesses to avoid detection.

However, patient hackers can use stealthy methods with online attacks. For example, they could use an automated tool to try logging in with a different password once every hour 24 hours until it finds a valid password. Another method is to try a single common password and cycle through a large list of usernames to find those users with that password. Yet another method is to take several common username/password combinations and try them across hundreds, or even thousands, of Web sites.

Online attacks are difficult but there are enough people with enough weak passwords that they will always yield results. The benefit of an online attack is that it is simple to launch a quick, anonymous attack against a web site or even a single account.

Offline attacks are more sophisticated, but when they are successful, they usually provide a huge windfall for the attacker. Offline attacks occur when an intruder is somehow able to obtain access to the database of password hashes. I explained earlier that password hashes are one-way functions and that they cannot be directly converted into passwords, but if someone can steal the hashes, they can perform an offline attack.

If someone can obtain password hashes, they can perform dictionary and brute-force attacks, essentially trying millions of passwords until they find the right one. These attacks are equivalent to trying every key on a huge key chain until you find the one that opens the lock. Because there is no system to enforce lockouts or other countermeasures, attackers are free to try as many passwords as they want for as long as they want. Because so many people have weak passwords, they are quite vulnerable to offline attacks. It is not uncommon for a hacker to obtain passwords for 50 percent of all hashes in just a matter of minutes.

Offline attacks usually involve taking a password, hashing that password, and then comparing it against the hash in the hash database. If the attacker's search finds a hash that matches, that means the attacker guessed a correct password.

The prerequisite for an offline attack is that the attacker must have already broken the system's security enough to obtain the database of password hashes. Sometimes this requires a sophisticated attack, but all too often, programmers or system administrators make mistakes that expose these hashes. In fact, it is often possible for a hacker to obtain password hashes using nothing more than a search engine such as Google.

Knowing what to search for, an attacker could search for vulnerable Web sites, obtain their hashes, and set their software to crack those hashes until they find an account to gain access. This is quite common in the porn hacking community where some individuals, the exploiters, obtain the hashes, and others, the crackers, use their software to crack them. Once these hashes are cracked, the attackers can trade or even sell large lists of passwords to others.

In the following sections, I describe a few of the online and offline methods that password crackers use.

Smart Guesses

The easiest method to gain your password is simply to guess it. Many hackers simply try the five most common passwords for a particular system. They might also try a blank password and a password that is the same as the user-name. If they get nothing they just move on to the next account and keep trying until they find the accounts with weak passwords. These methods work by attempting them on large numbers of accounts. Hackers often use automated tools that allow for large-scale attacks.

If someone knows you, that person might try entering passwords related to your personal life—for instance, trying the name of your girlfriend or prized sports car. Someone might happen to know one or more passwords you have used elsewhere and try those. This technique is the most basic form of attack, but it is still very effective.

Dictionary Attacks

Dictionary attacks are usually offline attacks against a password, but they can also be effective online when used correctly. A dictionary attack involves taking a list of words, often a dictionary, and trying every word until a valid password is found. To facilitate dictionary attacks, many wordlists are available on the Internet at Web sites such as http://sourceforge.net/projects/wordlist.

Many software tools are available to automate dictionary attacks against various systems. Most of these tools are smart enough to try simple variants of dictionary words, such as words followed by one or two numbers or simple letter substitutions.

Brute-Force Attacks

Brute-force attacks are more tedious but more complete versions of dictionary attacks. Brute-force attacks also involve trying millions of passwords, but they work by trying every combination of every letter and every punctuation symbol until a password is found. This type of attack could potentially take years to succeed, so it is often used as a last resort. Brute-force attacks are slow and time-consuming, but still quite common. I will cover brute-force attacks in more detail in the Chapter 4, "Character Diversity: Beyond the Alphabet."

Rainbow Tables

Offline attacks work by hashing millions of passwords in order to find hashes that match those of the target. Rainbow tables facilitate these attacks by pre-computing the hashes for billions of passwords. These tables take a very long time to generate, but once you have the tables, you can crack a large number of passwords in a matter of seconds.

To make things easier, the Shmoo Group has computed these tables and made them freely available on its Web site, http://rainbowtables.shmoo.com/.

Rainbow tables are significant because they immediately make every password that contains fewer than 15 characters immediately vulnerable if exposed to an offline attack.

Social Engineering

Sometimes a hacker can get your password simply by asking for it. Although it is perhaps the oldest trick in the book, this technique is still quite effective.

Hackers might pose as help desk or support staff and try to trick you into revealing your password. They might send you an e-mail claiming that your eBay or PayPal account is suspended, providing a place for you to enter your password. They might even take advantage of your greed by providing some trick to get rich quick or take advantage of others and in the process take advantage of you.

The best defense for these types of attacks is simply never giving out your password to anyone, no matter who you think they are.

Other Techniques

Hackers have many techniques at their disposal. They can use *key loggers* to record every keystroke you type on your keyboard. They can use *sniffers*, specialized tools to watch network traffic to obtain passwords sent over the network unencrypted. They can exploit vulnerabilities in Web browsers to obtain cookies that might contain authentication information. They could even hold a gun to your head and just ask for your password. The techniques are numerous, and they constantly evolve.

Winning the Numbers Game

The most effective way to defeat password crackers is to use strong passwords. If your password is long enough, random enough, and does not contain personal information, obtaining your password using the most common techniques would be extremely difficult. A strong password is essential in this world.

Fortunately, the numbers can be on your side.

Most password-cracking techniques involve a trade-off of time or CPU power. Searching through billions of passwords while trying to find the right one takes time. However, computers are growing more powerful every year. It is not unusual for a password-cracking tool to be able to search through a million passwords per second— almost a hundred billion passwords a day.

This processing power means that you aren't safe enough forcing attackers to try a billion passwords; you need to force them to try a trillion, or a thousand trillion. The numbers are your only defense.

You need to make cracking your password so difficult that no one will have the patience or resources to do so. Throughout this book, I will explain how to gird yourself with this protection, but for now I will explain why the numbers are so important.

The complexity of your password determines how long it will take someone to crack your password. Your password should never be simple enough to be vulnerable to a dictionary attack, and you should hide your password among a thousand trillion other possible passwords. Thus, your password must comprise at least 10 characters and contain more than just lower-case letters.

A number like a trillion is hard to imagine. Here are some facts to put it into perspective:

- A trillion (1,000,000,000,000) is a thousand billions, at least in most English-speaking countries. (In the United Kingdom, Ireland, Australia, and New Zealand a 1 followed by 12 zeroes is a called a billion).

- A light year—the distance it takes for light to travel in a year—is about 6 trillion miles.

- The moon has about 81,000 trillion tons of mass.

- The world?s 200 richest people have an estimated combined wealth of more than $1.3 trillion

- It would take just over a trillion pennies to fill the entire Empire State Building.

On the other hand, IBM's Blue Gene/L supercomputer can operate at speeds of over 280 *terfaflops*, an abbreviation for a trillion floating-point operations per second. A trillion is a large number, but computing power can shrink it quite quickly.

Your password needs to be a single penny in a thousand Empire State Buildings full of pennies (see Figure 2.2). That is your only protection.

Figure 2.2 Make Your Password Like a Penny in a Thousand Empire State Buildings Full of Pennies

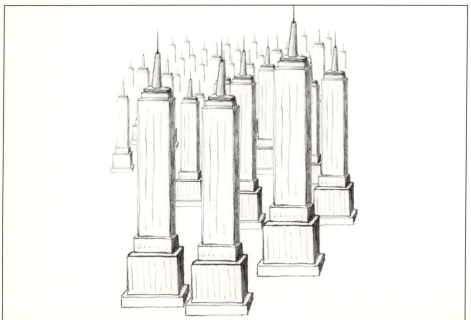

For someone to try cycling through a thousand trillion passwords, it would take them a very, very long time—at least using today's technology. If someone used a hundred computers, at the rate of a million passwords per second, expecting to crack your password on average halfway through, the time needed to crack your password would be 317,098 years.

Summary

Password security depends greatly on your own attitude and caution about security. If you are careless with your passwords, you can probably count on an attacker stealing it some day. You must also be careful about what information you reveal about yourself. Always remember that just about anything you post in a public Internet forum could be indexed by search engines such as Google.com and archive sites such as Archive.org. This information could be around for years, even decades. Old Web sites that you no longer have may still exist in some cache somewhere, available to anyone who wants to gather information about you. Numerous public sources of information also might reveal private information about you. Your e-mail address is probably already scattered throughout the Internet.

Always use caution when you publish any information on the Internet and consider the ramifications. Web sites such as eBay encourage sellers to create a profile page where you can provide personal information about yourself, your family, your pets, and your interests. This information can be useful for a hacker if your password is somehow related to that information. Furthermore, someone could use a Web site like eBay to determine what kinds of things you have bought or sold in the past. Again, this is all information that an attacker might use against you.

Be smart about what you publish and be smart about your password. This book should give you the ideas and techniques necessary to build strong, unbreakable passwords.

Chapter 3

Is Random Really Random?

Solutions in this chapter:

- **Randomness**
- **Compensating for Lack of Randomness**

Randomness

Password security essentially revolves around one basic strategy: creating a password that no one else can predict (or guess) within a reasonable amount of time, and then changing it regularly to continually make it difficult to predict.

It is not easy to "intentionally" be unpredictable. Human beings have to struggle to be random and sometimes in the process end up being even more predictable. Randomness—the most important aspect of password security—is what we struggle with the most.

Part of the problem is that we generally have a poor concept of randomness—it is difficult to define. For example, when we gamble on a certain slot machine for a period of time with no luck, we tend to move on to another, perhaps luckier, machine. When someone scores a huge jackpot on a machine, they believe that it is now *spent* and move on to another machine. Gamblers talk so much about winning streaks, being hot or cold, and payout averages that they are almost superstitious about randomness. However, the flaw in this is that random has no preference and no memory. Randomness does not track statistics and is completely unpredictable. Sure, if you track enough slot machines over a long enough period of time they will pay off, but a slot machine could get three jackpots in a row or never hit a jackpot. Randomness does not know the difference—there is no trend or bias.

NOTE

I have heard gamblers theorize that gaming companies design slot machines specifically to benefit the casinos that own them, by somehow manipulating the randomness of the machine. However, this could not be farther from the truth. These companies go to great lengths to ensure that their machines are as random as possible; inconsistencies in their randomness could potentially be exploited. Kevin Mitnick writes about this in his book *The Art of Intrusion* (Wiley, ISBN: 0-7645-6959-7). In this book, he describes how four individuals found weaknesses in and exploited the random number generators in slot machines for their own benefit.

If it has been 100 years since the last 100-year storm, do you think one is due any day? Additionally, after that storm, do you think people should worry about the next one?

We also have trouble recognizing whether data is random or not. Consider the first 50 digits of the value of *Pi*: 3.14159265358979323846264338327950288419716939937. The number looks random, but if you looked at it long enough you might see some patterns. Is it truly random? If you had a computer generating random numbers repeatedly, it would eventually produce the number that represents Pi, although it might take decades to happen.

NOTE

Pi is such a complex number that many people consider it close to being random. There is a 63 percent chance of finding the digits of your birthday in the first 100 million digits of Pi (see *http://www.angio.net/pi/piquery*).

Likewise, you may have heard that if you had enough monkeys randomly typing on typewriters they would eventually produce the entire works of Shakespeare. As unlikely as this seems, does it mean the works of Shakespeare are random? Are dice random? Is the static on a TV screen random? Are cloud formations random? Is your password random?

What Is Randomness?

Randomness is a strange concept. We do not really know what true randomness is. We call something random when we see no apparent pattern in a sequence. For example, we can see that the sequence 1, 2, 3, 4, 5 is not random because we see a pattern. We can easily speculate how the sequence would continue. The sequence 10, 100, 1000, 10000 also has a recognizable pattern. On the other hand, the sequence 93, 2, 75, 49, 36 has no apparent pattern and therefore, we cannot predict the next number in the sequence. If there is no formula or pattern we can use to reproduce the sequence, then we consider that sequence random. In other words, randomness is the absence of order.

The lack of order, however, does not guarantee that something is random. A sequence is only random if there is no way it can be reproduced given any circumstances or information (e.g., the value of Pi appears random but there is a specific method used to reproduce those digits).

It is difficult to actually determine if a sequence is truly random; therefore we look at several properties of a sequence to determine its randomness:

- **Even Distribution** An equal probability of distribution over the entire set of data.

- **Unpredictability** Any one piece of data has no relationship to any previous data and provides no information about the data to follow.

- **Uniqueness** It would be extremely rare to randomly produce the same sequence of data more than once. The longer the sequence, the more unique it becomes.

These three properties deem random data impossible to guess, therefore making randomness a vital element for strong passwords.

Unfortunately, completely random passwords are very difficult to remember and even if we could remember them, creating them would be a complicated task.

Even Distribution

Even distribution means that before producing a random sequence of data, there is an equal probability of all possible outcomes. Before you roll a dice, there is an equal chance of landing on any one of its sides. Because of this even distribution, we can assume that after a long period of time, randomly generated data will cover the entire data set.

Imagine a lawn sprinkler (see Figure 3.1). As it sprays out droplets of water, it is impossible to predict which blade of grass will be hit with any particular drop of water. Before any drop of water leaves the sprinkler, there is an equal probability that any blade of grass within range of the sprinkler will receive water. Likewise, if you run the sprinkler long enough, water will eventually cover all of the grass within the sprinkler's range. Furthermore, you can normally expect that all of the grass will receive approximately the same amount of water over a period of time, because the distribution is non-biased.

Figure 3.1 A Lawn Sprinkler

Human languages are not random; therefore, the passwords derived from these languages are also not random. If we counted the appearance of each different character in each different password, we would see that we are far from random. Figure 3.2 shows the actual distribution of password characters for over three million passwords. The figure clearly shows that most people prefer lowercase letters and some numbers in their passwords. If passwords were truly random, there would be a more even distribution like that in Figure 3.3, which represents passwords created by a computer random character generator.

Figure 3.2 Distribution of Password Characters

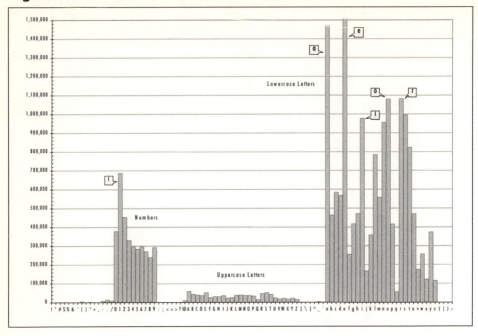

It is important to note that "even distribution" does not always mean that random data is evenly distributed. There is only the *possibility* that the data will be evenly distributed. The distribution in Figure 3.3 is not perfectly flat, because even distribution is the statistical average after many samples. If you flip a coin 100 times, you will not get exactly 50 heads and 50 tails. You may have 46 heads and 54 tails, or you may have 52 heads and 48 tails. The more you flip the coin, the closer it will get to the average of 50 percent each. Even distribution means that random data can take any format—evenly spread out, clustered, or a combination of the two. If you flip a coin, there is always the possibility of getting heads five times in a row. One outcome is just as likely as any other outcome.

Figure 3.3 Passwords Created by a Random Character Generator

Unpredictability

What makes something truly random is having no prior knowledge to help determine what data will appear next in a random sequence. In the English language, it is extremely rare for the letter "Q" to be followed by anything but the letter "U"; therefore, the sequences of letters in English phrases are quite predictable and therefore not truly random. With perfect randomness, every piece of data is completely independent of every other piece of data. There is no memory and there is no relationship between any two pieces of data.

The English language is full of repetition, which is helpful when communicating, but also makes it predictable. Some letters are used more than others and some words are used more than others. Figure 3.2 demonstrates the uneven distribution of letter passwords, which are largely based on dictionary words.

This is why many security professionals recommend using completely random sequences of letters rather than English words—they are just too predictable.

You can gauge the unpredictability of a sequence by measuring its *entropy*. Entropy is the measure of disorder, or lack of information. Information density is basically a measure of how much redundancy there is in a data sequence.

To illustrate entropy, consider this phrase from William Shakespeare's Hamlet, "To be, or not to be." It is a short phrase made up of 20 characters, but how much information does it really contain? You might say that there are 20 pieces of information, but if you look closely, there really are only six unique letters in this phrase. Moreover, if you look closer, you might notice that there are only two word pairs, "to be" and "or not." Perhaps you could argue that the phrase is made up of only two pieces of information. You could even argue that the entire phrase is so common (Googling for that phrase turns up 2.3 million results) that the entire phrase is a single piece of information.

It turns out that the English language is estimated to be 50 percent redundant. In other words, you could leave out half of the letters in a sentence and it could still be understood. That also means that a password based on English words must be twice as long as a completely random password to have equivalent entropy.

Uniqueness

If you take a sequence of random data (e.g., ten random characters), you have a small chance of repeating the same 10-character sequence twice. However, as the length increases, there is a smaller chance of repetition. That is why it is so difficult to randomly guess a valid credit card number. There are so many possible variations of credit card numbers that for every valid number there are potentially millions of unused numbers. Because random numbers are so evenly distributed and because there is no relationship between any two characters, chances are that truly random sequences will rarely repeat.

A lack of randomness is a huge weakness with most passwords. There simply are not enough different words, even if you consider all common languages and if you add numbers to the end of each word. Eight lowercase letters arranged in any order could potentially produce 26^8 or 208,827,064,576 possible words. However, in the entire English language, there are only about 17,000 eight-letter words, of which only about 500 are commonly used. That means that for every eight-letter English word there are more than 12 million eight-letter combinations that are not English words.

Because most passwords are not evenly distributed, unpredictable, or unique, they are vulnerable to attack and provide little security. Rather than being evenly distributed, most passwords are clustered together in groups of similar passwords.

To demonstrate the lack of randomness in passwords, compare the entire land surface of the United States to the total possible variations of eight characters that you can type on a typical keyboard. The surface area represents the total number of passwords, only considering passwords of exactly eight characters. Now imagine millions of people picking a one-centimeter spot anywhere in the entire United States to represent their password. Based on actual password data, despite the fact that they had the entire area of the United States to utilize, 98 percent of all passwords would fit into an area about 36 inches square.

If you are trying to crack passwords, this is wonderful news. You do not have a huge space to search because most passwords are in approximately the same location.

Human Randomness

Because humans have such a poor understanding of randomness, it is very difficult for us to produce randomness on our own. Try this yourself. On a computer keyboard, type a long string of random characters. As you type, you will notice that it is difficult producing data that would be considered truly random. Chances are you will have many *asdf* and *uiop* sequences in your typing.

To make matters worse, the harder you try to be random, the more predictable you become (e.g., you might purposely avoid any redundancy or obvious patterns and as a result create other predictable patterns. Consider the "guess-which-hand" game. Put an object in one of your hands, place both hands behind your back, and ask a child to guess which hand the object is in. At that point, their guess will be somewhat random. Play it again and this time their guess is largely based on the result of the last game (e.g., if they correctly guessed the left hand last time, they might try guessing the left hand again the next time). On the other hand, they might be smarter and expect you to switch so they guess the right hand. Play the game repeatedly and you will see patterns develop in both your selection and the child's response.

If you give someone a handful of pennies and ask them to spread the pennies out randomly on a table, you will find that at first glance, most people seem capable of arranging the pennies in a manner that looks random. But, often if you look closely, there is some pattern that defines the randomness (e.g., although the pennies look randomly arranged, the spaces between each penny might actually be the same (see Figure 3.4). In our attempt to create randomness, we still fall back to some pattern.

Figure 3.4 A Seemingly Random Arrangement of Pennies

Our lack of randomness is evident in our passwords. We tend to use words close to our personal lives or our environment. We pick numbers and words that mean something to us rather than selecting from the entire range of available words. We might try to open a dictionary to a random page and pick a word, but even where we open the book or what part of the page we select from has some bias.

Machine Randomness

It turns out that computers have their own problems when it comes to creating randomness. You cannot just tell registers and circuits to pick a series of truly random characters. A computer needs precise instructions, even when it comes to knowing which random character to produce. As a result, computers use what is called a Pseudo Random Number Generator (PRNG). Pseudo random numbers are not truly random, but rather an algorithm that creates numbers that appear to be random, but that are actually a predictable sequence of numbers. The key to the randomness is the *seed*, a value used to initiate the random sequence. If you know the seed, you can reproduce the sequence of random numbers.

To address this, computers use sophisticated methods to seed their random number generators and to gather random data. These can be based on time, environmental factors, or user activity with a keyboard or mouse. Some have even taken it further in their quest for true randomness. Table 3.1 shows some publicly accessible sources of random data and the method used to produce this data

Table 3.1 Publicly Accessible Sources of Random Data

URL	Source of Entropy
www.random.org	Atmospheric noise collected with a radio
www.fourmilab.ch/hotbits	Radioactive decay of Krypton-85
www.lavarnd.org	Random noise from a CCD camera

Compensating for Lack of Randomness

Now that I have demonstrated how insufficient our supply of randomness is, I will tell you that it does not matter so much when it comes to passwords. This is because we can compensate for our lack of true randomness with a few tricks that work well for passwords.

I stated earlier that random sequences have an even distribution of characters. In other words, they guarantee there will not be an *uneven* selection of characters. As Figure 3.2 shows, we are uneven in our character selections but we do not have to be perfect to thwart password crackers. In fact, we only need a few dispersed characters to gain the same benefit. Just the possibility of having a few numbers or symbols anywhere in a password makes things harder for a cracker. There does not need to be an even distribution of characters, just enough to force the crackers to anticipate and check for them every time.

To illustrate this, consider the widely recognized game of Rock, Papers, Scissors (RPS). The game is very simple. Two players simultaneously select one of three hand gestures to represent rock, paper, or scissors. The winner is determined by these three rules:

1. Rock smashes scissors.
2. Scissors cut paper.
3. Paper covers rock.

Every gesture chosen has an equal chance of winning, losing, or drawing an opponent's gesture. RPS is a fascinating study of randomness, because rounds of RPS are basically series of random combinations. It has long been considered a fair method of selection or elimination.

At first glance, the results of any RPS round seem quite random and should even out over time, just like a coin toss or rolling dice. There are three choices for each player and each player has the opportunity to choose any of these three in an unpredictable manner.

Strangely enough, this is not case. There are strategies and there are people who consistently win the game using these strategies. There are even competitions and world championships.

If you play against Stanford University's automated Roshambot (*http://chappie.stanford.edu/~perry/roshambo/*) long enough, odds are you will find yourself losing to the software program. The computer clearly has a better strategy than most humans do.

There are many advanced RPS strategies, called *gambits*, which go by names such as "Scissor Sandwich" and "Paper Dolls." A gambit is a series of three throws selected with strategic intent. There are only 27 possible gambits in RPS, and eight in particular that are most commonly used. These so-called "Great Eight" gambits are as follows:

- Avalanche (Rock–Rock–Rock)

- Bureaucrat (Paper–Paper–Paper)

- Crescendo (Paper–Scissors–Rock)

- Dénouement (Rock–Scissors–Paper)

- Fistfull o' Dollars (Rock–Paper–Paper)

- Paper Dolls (Paper–Scissors–Scissors)

- Scissor Sandwich (Paper–Scissors–Paper)

- Toolbox (Scissors–Scissors–Scissors)

Experienced RPS players chain these moves into larger combination strategies. It is interesting to note that of the above gambits, only two use all three gestures. In fact, there is not an even distribution of the three gestures among the great eight. Rock appears six times (25 percent), Paper appears ten times (42 percent), and Scissors appears eight times (33 percent). Yet these techniques work.

If you play RPS against someone who rarely, if ever, chooses Rock, you will still have to anticipate that they possibly could and therefore play as if they would suddenly change their strategy. The same is the case with passwords. Your password does not need to be a perfect mix of letters, numbers, and punctuation without any repetition to be effective. There just has to be enough diversity for an attacker to always have to consider that possibility.

Less Predictable

We are probably incapable of true unpredictability on our own, but that is okay. True unpredictability means that every piece of information in your password is independent of every other and that you cannot use partial knowledge of a password to predict the remainder. That means that a truly unpredictable password would be a stream of unrelated characters, which is always difficult to remember. On the other hand, as you try to improve the memorability of your password, you will undoubtedly increase predictability.

Fortunately, as explained in Chapter 2, "Meet the Opponent," cracking passwords is an all or nothing pursuit. If someone tries to guess your password, they will be either 100 percent right or 100 percent wrong; there is no in-between. The computer will never tell them that the password they entered is 20 percent incorrect. With that in mind, a password does not have to be completely unpredictable to be effective. All it takes is enough unpredictability to prevent the password from being vulnerable to attack. You can use the rest of the characters to help you remember the password.

Here are some examples of completely unpredictable passwords:

- 3Kja&Ey#
- u?7h%dPW
- @bx8R2k$

On the other hand, here are some better passwords that use unpredictability just enough to keep the password strong without sacrificing the ability to remember them:

- WhitenEighteen
- Fast+rocketing+
- creepy—FIVES

- Imp ort.ant
- cake and tape

If you look at these passwords, you can see that many individual characters might be predictable, based on the characters before and after. However, the password as a whole is not predictable and therefore sufficiently strong.

More Unique

There is no such thing as "more unique"—something is either unique or it is not, there are no levels of uniqueness. However, when it comes to passwords, you need to think in terms of being *more* unique. By this I mean that your password should be so different from anything else that even a super-fast cracking tool that tried every imaginable permutation still would not come across your password. This is where most people fail. Consider the following list of actual passwords based on the word *dragon*:

$dragon, 01dragon, 108dragons, 12dragon, 13dragon, 19dragon, 1Dragon, 1dragon1, 1dragon2, 1Dragons, 21dragon, 2dragon, 2dragon5, 34dragon, 3dragon3, 44dragon, 4dragon, 4dragon4, 5dragons, 64dragon, 666dragon, 69dragon, 6dragon9, 77dragon, 79dragon, 7dragon2, 7dragon9, 7dragons, 87dragon, 89dragon, 96dragon, 9dragon, 9dragons, balldragon, bdragon, blackdragon, bluedragon, darkdragon, Drag0n, Drag0n11, drag0n21, drag0n22, drag0n42, drag0n8, drag0n89, drag0nFF, Drag0ns1, dragon, dragon*p, dragon@, dragon, Dragon0, dragon00, dragon01, dragon01p, dragon02, dragon03, dragon04, dragon05, dragon0512, Dragon06, dragon07, Dragon1, dragon10, dragon101, dragon11, dragon116, dragon12, dragon123, dragon1232, dragon13, dragon14, dragon15, dragon15a, dragon16, dragon17, dragon18, dragon19, dragon1966, dragon1976, Dragon2, dragon20, dragon21, dragon22, dragon23, dragon25, dragon26, dragon27, dragon28, dragon29, dragon31, dragon32, dragon323, dragon33, dragon3317, dragon34, dragon35, dragon36, dragon369, dragon37, dragon3x, Dragon4, dragon42, dragon43, dragon44, dragon45, dragon46, dragon47, dragon49, dragon4ever, dragon4m, dragon5, dragon50, dragon53, dragon54, Dragon5fist, dragon5m, dragon6, dragon60, dragon62, dragon63, Dragon64, dragon65, dragon66, dragon666, Dragon69, dragon6c, Dragon6f, Dragon7, dragon70, dragon71, dragon713, dragon72, dragon73, dragon74, dragon75, dragon76, dragon761, dragon77, dragon8, dragon81, Dragon85, dragon87, dragon88, dragon89974, dragon9, dragon93, DRAGON95, dragon96, dragon97, DRAGON98, dragon99, Dragona, dragonar, dragonas, dragonass, dragonb, dragonball, dragonballs, dragonballz, dragonbeam, dragonbone, dragonbreath, Dragonbz, dragonclaw, dragondb, dragone, dragone1, dragonef, Dragoner, dragones, dragoney, dragonf, Dragonf1, dragonfang, dragonfi, dragonfighter, dragonfire, dragonfire12, dragonfl, dragonflly1, dragonfly, dragonfly1, dragongod, dragongt, dragongu, dragonha, dragonhe, dragonhu, dragonj2, dragonj3, dragonja, dragonjd, dragonki, dragonl, dragonlady, dragonlance, dragonlord, dragonlords, dragonlvr, dragonman, DragonMaster, dragonn, dragonnes, dragonnor, Dragonor, dragonorb, dragonos, dragonov, dragonp, dragonpa, dragonphoenix3, dragonR, dragonrage, dragonrat, dragonrd, dragonri, dragonron, dragons, dragons1, dragons2, dragons52, dragons531, dragons7, dragons9, dragonsf, dragonsign, dragonsl, dragonslayer, dragonsp, Dragonss, Dragonst, dragonsy, dragonsz, dragont, dragonta, dragontale, dragontalep, dragontR, dragonus, dragonw, dragonwa, dragonwi, Dragonwing1, dragonwo, dragonwolf, Dragonwyng, dragonx, dragonx1, dragonz, dragonz1, Dragonz4, dragonzz, firedragon, gothik_dragon, Greendragon, hcdragon, icedragon, mydragon, pdragon, pdragon9, pendragon, ratdragon9, rbdragon, rdragon, reddragon, redragon, sdragon, sdragon739, sexdragon, SilkDragon, silverdragon, snapdragon, Tdragon, tsdragon, wdragon, wdragon1, wikeddragon, xdragon, xdragon3x, yearofthedragon

If you study the list for a few moments, you will see that it would not be difficult for a computer to try 90 percent of those variants in very little time. While these passwords are unique, most of them are not different enough to resist exposure to a smart password cracker. You should also notice how consistent and predictable these passwords are.

Nevertheless, you might also notice that there are a few passwords that are somewhat less predictable than the rest. Passwords like *gothik_dragon* and *dragonphoenix3* are more unique in the sense that it would take many more permutations of the word *dragon* to arrive at those passwords. These passwords hint at the key to uniqueness: make your passwords longer. A long, unique password has much less chance of being cracked than a short unique password. It is simple math; the more characters you include in your password, the more opportunity you have to make it unique. In addition, since you already know that English is about 50 percent redundant, you should expect to make your passwords twice as long as you normally would.

Sure, humans are poor sources of randomness, but with a little help and some simple strategies, we can make up for that and have very strong passwords. The next two chapters, "Character Diversity: Beyond the Alphabet" and "Password Length: Making It Count," demonstrate ways that we can increase the distribution, unpredictability, and uniqueness of our passwords.

Chapter 4

Character Diversity: Beyond the Alphabet

Solutions in this chapter:

- **Understanding Character Space**

Understanding Character Space

A number of years ago I did technical support for a large PC manufacturer. One day I took a call from a customer who complained that his floppy drive would not accept his floppy disk. I have received similar calls many times in the past, and I knew he just wasn't inserting it correctly. After struggling for a few minutes and failing to get him to orient the disk properly, I decided on a new strategy.

I instructed the customer to hold the floppy disk and try to insert it. If it didn't fit in the slot, I told him to rotate it clockwise one turn and try it again. After trying all four sides, I had him flip it over and try the next four sides. I figured that there are only eight possible ways you could insert the disk, so he would eventually find the correct one. He eventually got it, but it somehow took him nine attempts to get it right!

This was essentially a *brute-force* method of finding the correct way to insert the disk. If you try every possible direction for inserting the disk, you will eventually find the correct one. In this case, it would take a maximum of eight attempts (or maybe nine for some people) to find the correct direction.

At the beginning of the last school year, my son wanted to ride his bike to school but he forgot the combination for his bicycle lock. I looked at the lock and saw that there were three dials, each one with the digits 0 through 9 (see Figure 4.1). Immediately I thought I might be able to discover the code using the brute-force method. To do this, I set all digits to 0 and pulled on the lock. It didn't open so I tried 001, then 002, then 003, and so on. I knew that the combination was somewhere between 000 and 999—a thousand possible combinations.

Figure 4.1 A Bicycle Lock Having Three Dials, Each with 10 Numbers, Giving the Lock 1,000 Possible Combinations

Of course, I wouldn't have to always try all thousand combinations. It could just as likely be the first one I tried as the last. Statistically, there would be a 50 percent chance of me finding the correct combination halfway through, so I'd probably end up trying around 500 combinations. That might be a lot of work but it certainly is doable. I could just work my way through the possible combinations while watching TV, lying in bed, sitting on the toilet, or whenever I find spare time on my hands.

This is another example of a brute-force attack. If you try every possible combination, you'll eventually find the right one. In fact, you're guaranteed to ultimately find the correct one if you're diligent enough.

Brute Force...

How I Eventually Cracked the Lock

It turned out that cracking my son's bicycle lock didn't take 1,000 attempts after all. I discovered a flaw in the lock's design. I found that once I correctly set the leftmost number, I could slide the lock out one notch where the next dial stopped it. After I found the second number I could slide it out one more, and so on until the third number. This meant I could brute force one digit at a time—starting at 0 until I found the first digit, and then repeating the method for each dial thereafter. So there were a maximum of 10 solutions for each digit, for a total maximum of 30 attempts. It turns out I cracked the combination in about 15 attempts.

The correct way to have designed the lock is to have required all three digits to be correct before you could move the lock at all.

One thousand possible combinations is a lot, but imagine a bicycle lock that not only had the numbers 0 through 9 but also had the letters A through Z on each dial. That means there would be 36 possible settings for each dial. If there were three dials, each with 36 possible values, that would be a total of 36^3 or 46,656 possible combinations. Simply by making the dials bigger, we made the lock's combination much more difficult to crack. The more values we can fit on each dial, the longer it would take to try all the combinations.

If we could fit every character available on a standard English keyboard on to each dial, then we could increase the number of possible combinations to more than 850,000, with just three (very large) dials. So while someone might be willing to try 1,000 combinations, few bikes would be worth the time put in to trying 850,000 possible solutions.

Cracking passwords using the brute force method means you try every possible value for each character position in the password until you find the correct password. For a five-character password, a cracker might start with *aaaaa* and go through every possible combination up to *zzzzz*. Obviously, this is a lot of permutations but there are specialized password cracking software applications that can rapidly try all possible passwords from *aaaaa* to *zzzzz* in a matter of seconds.

TIP

In reality, many automated password cracking tools do not go through each letter alphabetically, but rather start with the most common letters based on character frequency. Some tools are smart enough to adjust these character frequencies based on passwords it has already cracked.

To make things more difficult for password crackers, we use the same strategy as increasing the number of values on each dial of the bicycle lock. In other words, instead of using just lowercase letters for your password, you should use numbers, uppercase letters, punctuation, and so on. The next time you go to set a password and the system says you need numbers or punctuation in your password, essentially all you're doing is using a bigger dial. The bigger the dial, the longer it takes to brute force your password.

TIP

On most systems, passwords are case-sensitive. This means that it distinguishes between uppercase and lowercase letters, so the password *Apple* is not the same as *apple*. This is good because it allows more possible values for each character of your password.

This concept applies to just about anything you can brute force. For example, say you borrowed someone's key ring but do not know what key will work on a particular lock. Clearly, the greater the number of keys on the ring, the longer it will take for you to find the correct one.

Password Permutations

Most people underestimate the number power of *permutations*. This is perhaps because we see them more as *combinations*, which are mathematically different. Combinations refer to all possible selections from a pool of items where the order is not important. Permutations are the same thing, except that they take into account the order, allowing for more possible results.

Imagine, for example, a simple lottery game where you pick any three numbers from 0 to 9. You win if you match any of the winning numbers in any order. Suppose that you pick the numbers 1, 2, and 3 so if they draw out a 2, then a 1, then a 3, you are a winner. If they draw the numbers 3, then 2, and then 1, you are also a winner. In fact, given three numbers from 0 through 9, there are only 220 different combinations so you would always have a 1-in-220 chance of winning. This is called a combination.

I'll spare you the detailed math involved (see http://en.wikipedia.org/wiki/Combinations_and_permutations for the full explanation), but the formula for this is

$$\frac{(n + r - 1)!}{r!(n - 1)!}$$

Where n is the pool of numbers from which you can select and r is the quantity available. In this example, if you worked it out, it would come out to 220.

If you consider the order in which the numbers are drawn, the odds of winning decrease dramatically. Suppose that the lottery has a jackpot that you win if you match all three numbers in the exact order in which they were drawn (see Figure 4.2). And since we are comparing all this to passwords, suppose that any number could be drawn more than once. That means that the possible permutations are 10 numbers times 10 numbers times 10 numbers, or 10^3, or 1,000.

Figure 4.2 In a Lottery If You Get a Win by Matching Any Three Numbers in Any Order, There Are 220 Possible Combinations. If Order Does Matter, Then There Are 1,000 Possible Permutations.

The difference between 220 and 1,000 is great, but to help you better understand the difference, let's look at how the numbers grow depending on how many numbers you can choose from, as Table 4.1 shows. If you increase the pool of numbers you can select from, the number of permutations increases dramatically.

Table 4.1 Increasing the Pool of Numbers Greatly Increases the Permutations

Selections	Combinations	Permutations
3	220	1,000
6	5,005	1,000,000
7	11,440	10,000,000
8	24,310	100,000,000
9	48,620	1,000,000,000
10	92,378	10,000,000,000
11	167,960	100,000,000,000
12	293,930	1,000,000,000,000
13	497,420	10,000,000,000,000
14	817,190	100,000,000,000,000
15	1,307,504	1,000,000,000,000,000

Iinstead of 0 through 9, if you could pick any three numbers between 0 and 15, it would result in 4,096 permutations. This number of permutations grows much faster than the number of combinations.

Just as with lottery numbers, the larger the pool of characters you use in your passwords, the more possible permutations there are. This can make a big difference in resisting a brute force attack.

Character Sets

Too many password policies seem random, rejecting one password but accepting a similar password for no obvious reason. A friend recently explained to me a new system that he has at his workplace. When you set a password, there is an interactive gauge that, as you type, rates your password as Poor, Average, Better, and Strong. He pointed out to me that he entered his typical password, the one he always uses, and it gave him a rating of Average. But to his surprise, he simply added an asterisk to the end of the password and it increased to a Strong rating. What *he* learned from this experience is that asterisks make your password stronger.

But that system is a bit misleading. It wasn't the asterisk itself that added to the password strength, but the fact that he pulled from a different *character set*.

NOTE

Johnny loved surfing the Web, and kept track of his passwords by writing them on Post-It notes. His mother noticed his Disney Online password was, "MickeyMinnieGoofyPluto," and asked why he chose such a long password. Johnny replied, "Because, they said it has to have at least four characters."

In password terms, a character set is a group of keyboard characters that someone might use in a password. The basic character sets are

- **Numbers** Digits 0 through 9
- **Lowercase letters** Lowercase letters from a through z
- **Uppercase letters** Uppercase letters from A through Z
- **Symbols** Other punctuation and symbols such as the tilde (~), asterisk (*), or equals sign (=).

Many systems try to evaluate the potential strength of your password by checking to see how many different character sets you use—the more the better.

When establishing a password policy, a system administrator might require that you use a mix of more than one character set in your password. In Windows, there is a standard password complexity setting that requires using characters from at least three character sets. If you get an error message saying that your password doesn't meet complexity requirements, it usually means it wants more character sets, so try adding some numbers and symbols. The following are some examples of using different character sets:

One Character Set:

- applepie
- 6565656

Two Character Sets:

- HappyCamper (uppercase and lowercase)
- notnothing! (lowercase and symbol)

Three Character Sets:

- 677Mustangs (uppercase, lowercase, numbers)
- wrong3@email.com (lowercase, symbols, number)

All Four Character Sets:

- Different-2day
- 4 Broken (shellfish)
- Www2.example.com

NOTE

Most of the automated brute-force tools that crackers use let you choose which characters to use in the attack. Most commonly, they will try only letters and numbers to keep the attack time reasonable. When they change this setting, they usually do so by character sets. Therefore, by using any character in a character set, you require the cracker to try all characters in that set.

Lowercase Letters

Most passwords consist of lowercase letters of the alphabet. More than 75 percent of all characters used in passwords are lowercase letters, and more than 60 percent of all passwords use all lowercase characters and nothing else. Lowercase letters are the basis for most passwords, but you should try to use other character sets in addition to your lowercase letters.

Lowercase letters are common simply because they are the easiest and fastest to type. This makes them useful when you make extra long passwords. In fact, you should think of lowercase letters as your main strategy to increase the bulk and complexity of your passwords.

Here are some examples of using lowercase letters creatively in your passwords:

- yer weather is colllder
- sitting at the mall in springville
- collidingwithatomss
- left at the firststoplight

Note how these passwords are all 20 characters or longer. They are easy to type and easy to remember. If you use passwords less than 15 characters, you should avoid using all lowercase letters and mix in other character sets.

Uppercase Letters

It is interesting to note that less than three percent of all passwords contain uppercase letters. Most of the time, uppercase letters appear only in the first or second character positions. In other words, most of these are capitalized words. Don't forget to use uppercase letters and be sure to use them unpredictably throughout your password.

The following shows some examples of using uppercase letters in your passwords:

- Evan the IV
- Call the FBI
- CRAVING.com
- Radio 99.3 KRPP
- whitefish.DLL

Numbers

Numbers are probably the most common method people use to increase the character sets in their passwords. The problem with numbers is that most people use them in such a predictable manner that they often do little to increase the strength of their passwords. You should still use numbers in your passwords, just be smart when you use them.

The most obvious weakness with using numbers is that there are only ten of them, which is only a small increase in character space. To make things worse, people tend to prefer some numbers over others. For example, most people use the number one much more than any other number. Figure 4.3 shows the breakdown of which numbers appear most frequently in passwords.

Figure 4.3 Number One Is the Most Common Number People Use in Their Passwords; Almost Twice As Much As Any Other Number

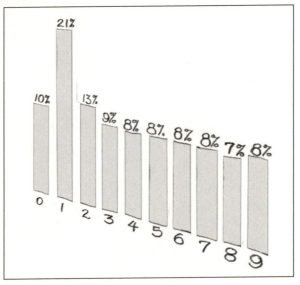

Looking at that chart, crackers could modify their brute-force strategy to only include the numbers one and two, which will get them a third of all passwords containing numbers.

In addition to using common numbers, people also tend to make patterns or sequences out of numbers. Examples of this are passwords that contain numeric strings such as 12345, 1212, 2005, 99, and so on. In fact, many of the top 500 passwords (shown in Chapter 9) are simple number sequences. Furthermore, if your password is *Fluffy12* and you are forced to change it, it is too easy to derive a predictable password such as *Fluffy13*. Avoid having more than 10 percent of your password be numbers, and avoid predictable numeric patterns.

The most common password pattern utilizing numbers is a dictionary word or name followed by one or two numbers, such as *cecil6*, *ford99*, *katie5*, or *broncos12*. You should avoid this pattern.

Almost a third of all passwords end in a number. Ten percent of all passwords end with the number one. If you use numbers in your password, try using them throughout your entire password and don't forget about the less popular numbers.

The following are some examples of how to use numbers in your passwords:

- 1515 Parsley Road
- 12 dozen dozens
- Channel 42 news
- Wasted 500 bucks
- Lost 7 socks
- Scoring 8 more points
- Go 50 miles on Rt. 80
- 1-800-go-NUTS

Symbols

Symbols are any characters that are not a number or a letter. This includes

- **Punctuation** Punctuation symbols for your language such as the period (.), comma (,), or apostrophe (").
- **Keyboard symbols** Non-punctuation symbols found on a standard keyboard, such as the tilde (~), backslash (\), or pipe (|).
- **Non-keyboard symbols** Printable characters that do not appear on a standard keyboard and require special key sequences to type, such as the copyright symbol (©), the diaeresis (¨), or the inverted question mark (¿).

■ **Nonprintable characters** Special control characters that do not print but that you can sometimes, rarely, use in passwords. This includes characters such as the backspace, enter, or tab.

Modern computer systems support a much greater character space beyond that of a typical keyboard. If you run the Character Map program by opening the Start Menu, selecting Program Files, and opening the Accessories menu, you will see that there are many different characters available, depending on the font. In fact, Microsoft's Arial font contains more than 65,000 different characters and symbols from a variety of languages. The support for these extended characters is referred to as Unicode.

You can access any of these characters by using the Alt key on your keyboard. For example, if you open WordPad, you can create a smiley-face character (☺) by holding down the Alt key, typing 9786 on the number pad, and then releasing the Alt key. Some typefaces may not support all these characters and will instead display a small box, but that does not matter because you never see your password anyway. Not all systems allow you to use these symbols in your passwords, but Windows will let you use any character code up to 65,535.

Using symbols, especially non-keyboard symbols, allows for the greatest possible character space. This is equivalent to the bicycle lock with 65,535 different positions on each dial. An eight-character password utilizing this entire character space allows for 340,240,830,764,391,000,000,000, 000,000,000,000,000 different permutations. Although that password is still guessable, the chances are that no one will ever guess it in a single lifetime.

However, that isn't to say that you should always use these characters. Keep in mind that typing these character codes using the Alt key and the number pad is slow and cumbersome. In fact, if you consider the number of keystrokes, it might be just as effective to make your password longer, as I explain in Chapter 5. Nevertheless, utilizing the full character space might be effective in high-security situations or with passwords that you rarely have to type manually.

Spaces are another underutilized password character. Most people don't realize that many systems do allow for spaces in passwords. Windows, for example, lets you use spaces not only within your password but also before and after your password. If you create a password combination followed by three spaces, someone else would have to do the same to gain access to your account—the spaces are part of your password.

Using spaces is a particularly effective strategy because:

- They are easy to remember. In fact, they are just spaces—nothing to remember at all.

- They encourage users to create longer, multiword passwords.

- They are easy and natural to type.

- They extend the character space beyond lowercase letters and numbers.

The only disadvantage I can think of for using spaces is that hitting the space bar makes a unique sound different than other keys. Perhaps using too many spaces would be revealing enough to a very clever attacker, who also happens to be within earshot when you type your password. This is hardly enough of a disadvantage to avoid spaces though.

TIP

Spaces can save you in surprising ways. I once instructed a client to use spaces in passwords. One day he wrote down the Administrator password on a piece of paper as he was setting up a new system. The paper went missing without him noticing that it was gone. He did, however, notice the next day that someone had tried and failed several times to log in to that Administrator account. The logs led him directly to the culprit, who was promptly fired.

So what saved my client from this intrusion? When he set the password, he ended it with a single space, which he obviously did not write down on paper. The other employee was trying the written password—without the trailing space.

Like numbers, people generally use symbols in a predictable manner. You are more likely to see periods, exclamation points, and question marks at the end of a password and are more likely to find hyphens, dashes, and commas between dictionary words. Dollar signs usually precede numbers, and percent signs will more likely follow numbers. The single most common use of symbols is a hyphen character in the fourth, fifth, and sixth character positions of a password, such as in passwords like *wall-orange* and *knot-five*.

The following are some examples of integrating punctuation and symbols into your passwords:

- Making $$$count
- 2+2+3 isn't five
- 1/2 the_meal
- Batman and/or/not Robin
- <h1>Introduction</h1>
- If (x=0) then
- C:\Program Files
- (999) dog-walk
- Smileys :) ;)
- Not! Again!?
- www.eatingcoldpizza-forbreakfast.com
- Staying "interconnected"

Summary

Character diversity is a key component of strong passwords. The purpose of using many different types of characters is to reduce the predictability and weakness of your passwords. Using numbers, uppercase letters, and symbols, if employed properly, can enhance the creativity and uniqueness of your passwords.

You want your password to be unique. In fact, you want them so unique that it would be unlikely for anyone else to have that very same password. Increasing the types of characters you use greatly increases your chances of building those unique passwords.

Chapter 5

Password Length: Making It Count

Solutions in this chapter:

- **Benefits of Long Passwords**
- **Building Longer Passwords**

Introduction

A couple of years ago, I was preparing to speak in front of a group at a conference. As I set up for the presentation, attendees slowly filled the room. I connected my laptop computer to the projector screen and logged in. This was my travel laptop. I password-protected my screensaver and set it to activate after just a few minutes of inactivity. And, of course, I had a very strong password.

As I set up, the screensaver activated several times, and each time I had to enter the password. As the audience filled, I started noticing occasional chuckles out in the audience that seemed to increase in volume each time. It took me a while, but I finally made the connection—they laughed each time I logged in to my laptop. My password at the time was 63 characters long. Apparently, they found that amusing.

But, if you know me, you know that I always use long passwords. Some people think I'm overly paranoid. Some people don't see how I can memorize passwords that long. However, using long passwords is the single most effective strategy in keeping your passwords secure. It is, in fact, so important that it can even make up for failing to follow any other password policy.

And they aren't that hard to remember.

The Benefits of Long Passwords

Long passwords are by no means the burden that most people imagine. Most people see long passwords as hard to remember and hard to type. The opposite is actually true. Long passwords certainly can be easier to remember, easier to type, but best of all, most difficult to break.

Easy to Memorize

The average adult in the U.S. has to remember 9.8 passwords, pin codes, or other bits of secret information. But for people who are around computers all day, such as IT professionals, they could easily find themselves having to keep track of 50 or more passwords. When you consider that many systems require you to regularly change your passwords (and you should on your own anyway), that's a lot of passwords to keep straight. Remembering all those passwords is obviously a big concern.

Sure, it seems logical that longer passwords might be more challenging to remember. But I say it's easier to remember long passwords than it is to remember short passwords—if you do them right.

Consider the following examples of short passwords that many security professionals would consider adequately secure based on widely accepted security best practices:

- Sup3rm@n
- Br9T&o2_
- Bl4CK-hAt
- Y*c77pw$
- 4W5T1UP

These might be fairly strong passwords, but you'd need some time to memorize them. If you studied those five passwords for a minute and then looked away, chances are you wouldn't be able to recall more than one or two of them. Go ahead and try it yourself. Now think about how much more difficult it would be if you had to remember a dozen different passwords like that, each of them unique. No wonder people hate passwords like these.

Now compare those with the following simpler, but longer passwords:

- skyisfalling
- in a coalmine.
- walnut-flavored
- orange toothpaste
- a hundred pesos

If you study this list for a minute, you'd quickly realize there's much less effort involved in memorizing these passwords, even though each is at least twice as long as those on the other list. Which ones would you rather have to memorize? It's interesting to note that the passwords on the second list are mathematically just as strong, (or stronger) as those on the first list. I'll explain just why this is true in more detail later in this chapter.

The actual number of characters in a password has nothing to do with our ability to memorize it. Our minds don't store information as individual characters; we see chunks of information and save those chunks, no matter how big they may be. For example, consider the phrase, *three blind-folded mice.* We don't memorize 18 letters, two spaces, and a dash. Instead, we memorize just four pieces of information—the four words in the phrase. We don't have to bother remembering the spaces, and perhaps not even the dash in the middle. That's the secret to long passwords—you may have a 24-character password but only have to remember a few pieces of information, and anyone can do that. In fact, if you visualize three blindfolded mice in your head, you really only have to remember one piece of information—that image in your head.

Part of the trick is that having more information actually helps you to remember it. If we left out any portion of the phrase *three blindfolded mice,* such as *three* _____ *mice,* we would still remember that word due to the context that the other information provides (see Figure 5.1).

Figure 5.1 When Remembering a Long Password, Such As **Three Blindfolded Mice,** It's Easy Just to Remember a Simple Mental Image.

An interesting side effect of this is that with long passwords you can record small reminders without having to record your entire password. For example, you might write down *blind mice* as a reminder until you are comfortable with the new password. This also works well in those cases where you have no choice but to share a password with others. If others forget the password, you can simply remind them that it is the *mice* password without having to say the whole password within earshot of others.

Humans brains have plenty of capacity to store and retain information and even a small child can easily memorize entire nursery rhymes or songs. The trick is to put things into a form that our brains can easily work with. Using long passwords gives you more space and opportunity to incorporate patterns or memorization techniques, such as those I'll describe later in this chapter.

Easy to Type

Again, this goes against conventional wisdom, but I also say that you can type longer passwords faster than you can shorter passwords. In addition, you can type them more accurately.

There is one provision, however, that you must already know how to type. If all you do now is hunt and peck, a long password is just a lot more hunting and a lot more pecking. But, if you can already type reasonably well, you will find yourself spending much less time entering long passwords.

My reasoning is based on what I explained earlier: people think in terms of words and phrases, not individual letters. It turns out that when we type on a keyboard we do the same thing. In our minds, we don't spell out each individual letter, we verbalize the words in our minds and our fingers just type that word. What slows us down is when we have to think about what we're typing. You might notice that as you type, you pause slightly between each sentence and even a little between each word. You type it as you say it in your head (see Figure 5.2).

Figure 5.2 When Typing, You Don't Type Individual Letters But Whole Words at a Time. Long Passwords Using Known Words Are Easier than Short Ones Composed of Random Characters.

If you have a password like *c@45Wa#B*, you tend to break it up into individual letters and hesitate as you think about, and type, each one. Furthermore, a password like *c@45Wa#B* requires reaching your fingers more across the keyboard and using extra keystrokes to hold down the shift key several times. Longer passwords, on the other hand, do not require as many unique character sets (such as symbols or numbers) so you can focus on low-ercase words you're more accustomed to typing.

Try it yourself. Time yourself typing passwords from the two lists in the previous section and you'll see the difference.

Another bonus with typing normal words is that you not only type them faster, but you tend to type them more accurately. The concept is still the same—people tend to type in words, as opposed to letters, and therefore are more accurate in doing so.

Harder to Crack

The greatest benefit of longer passwords is that password length is the single most important factor in building strong passwords. If your password is long enough, you really don't have to bother so much with numbers and symbols. Additionally, you don't have to worry about changing your password as frequently as you would with a shorter password.

There is a myth prevalent in the IT world that your password must be completely random and use a variety of character sets to be effective. Many system administrators would love seeing their users coming up with passwords like *7mv4?gHa* or *Y6+a4P#5*. While these passwords might be somewhat strong, this is not the only way to come up with strong passwords.

Often, administrators will try to force users to come up with strong passwords by implementing strong password requirements. If you've worked in an organization such as this, then you're well familiar with frustrating messages like that shown in Figure 5.3.

Figure 5.3: In an Effort to Force Users to Create Strong Passwords, Many Administrators Implement Complex and Confusing Password Policies.

There are two ways to increase the strength of your password: increase the character sets you use or increase the length of your password. In the previous chapter, I explained how you can use different character sets to make your password more resistant to brute-force attacks. Although this is an important strategy, it turns out that increasing the password length is just as effective, maybe even more effective. All it takes is adding a few characters to the length of a lowercase password to make it just as effective as a password that uses a mix of characters.

Consider this example: which do you think would have more possible combinations, rolling a 20-sided die just once or rolling a regular six-sided die three times? It turns out that a 20-sided die has only 20 possible outcomes, but rolling the six-sided die three times has 6^3, or 216 possible outcomes, as Figure 5.4 shows.

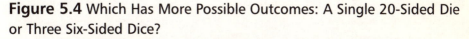

Figure 5.4 Which Has More Possible Outcomes: A Single 20-Sided Die or Three Six-Sided Dice?

If you compare this to passwords, Table 5.1 shows the difference between a password using all lowercase characters and a password that utilizes the full range of keyboard characters.

Table 5.1 To Strengthen a Password, You Can Increase Its Length or Make Use of More Character Sets

Length	Lowercase Only	All Keyboard Characters
3	17,576	857,375
4	456,976	81,450,625
5	11,881,376	7,737,809,375
6	308,915,776	735,091,890,625
7	8,031,810,176	69,833,729,609,375
8	208,827,064,576	6,634,204,312,890,620
9	5,429,503,678,976	630,249,409,724,609,000
10	141,167,095,653,376	59,873,693,923,837,900,000
11	3,670,344,486,987,780	5,688,000,922,764,600,000,000
12	95,428,956,661,682,200	540,360,087,662,637,000,000,000
13	2,481,152,873,203,740,000	51,334,208,327,950,500,000,000,000
14	64,509,974,703,297,200,000	4,876,749,791,155,300,000,000,000,000
15	1,677,259,342,285,730,000,000	463,291,230,159,753,000,000,000,000,000

According to this table, a seven-character password that incorporates the full range of keyboard characters is much more resistant to a brute-force attack than a seven-character lowercase password. However, a ten-character lowercase password has about twice as many permutations as the strong seven-character password. That means that a password such as *dozennozes* is more resistant to a brute-force attack than the password *J%3mPw6*.

> **NOTE**
>
> Keep in mind that the numbers shown in Table 5.1 grow exponentially, so the longer the password, the more characters you'll need to keep them equivalent.
>
> For example, a short password might just need one or two characters added; a long password might need five or more extra characters. Also, remember that these numbers mean absolutely nothing if you use easily guessable passwords such as dictionary words, the name of your cat, or your favorite sports team.

Sure, it's always better to incorporate symbols and numbers into your password, but if your password is long enough, say 20 characters or longer, it really doesn't make that much of a difference any more.

Did You Know?

Password Policies

If you're a system administrator and you enforce strict password policies, you may want to take a step back and rethink your strategy. A typical password policy might require a password of at least eight characters long and insist on the use of numbers and symbols. The problem with that policy is that you tend to get a whole lot of passwords like **'72Mustang** or **Michael-23**. While these aren't horrible passwords, they are somewhat predictable.

The bigger problem, however, is that users tend to get frustrated with password error messages, and many don't fully understand exactly how to avoid the message. Often, they just keep trying different passwords until one is finally accepted. So often, I hear users complain about their strict password policies at work—everyone hates them. Moreover, they resent the admins who enforce them.

There is an easier way, however, to ensure strong passwords without so much user frustration. Let them use whatever characters they want, even if they are all lowercase characters, but enforce a minimum password length that ensures adequate strength, say 15 characters or more. Users are more willing to enter longer passwords that always are accepted than struggle with entering the minimum number of character sets. Don't bother with complicated password policies, just enforce a minimum length.

On the same note, users also get frustrated with having to change their passwords every couple of months. Enforcing long passwords also helps make up for password aging policies; allowing users to stick with their passwords longer. Plus, users are more willing to come up with long passwords if they get to keep them for six months.

Other Security Benefits

Long passwords are mathematically more complex and therefore harder to crack, but there are also other security benefits to long passwords. The longer the password, the more likely it is to be different than any anyone else's password, and uniqueness means strong passwords. If you have a password of at least 12 characters, you eliminate nearly all common dictionary words, names, and most other common passwords. The longer your password, the less likely it will appear on any precompiled list.

Figure 5.5 shows the breakdown of word lengths of various lists. The solid line represents the lengths of more than two million actual passwords. Notice how few passwords exceed seven characters in length. By the time you get to 12 characters in length, you have eliminated most common words. Finally, a password of more than 20 characters is not likely to appear on any list.

Figure 5.5 A comparison of Word Lengths in Various Word Lists, Few Lists Contain Words Longer Than 12 Characters

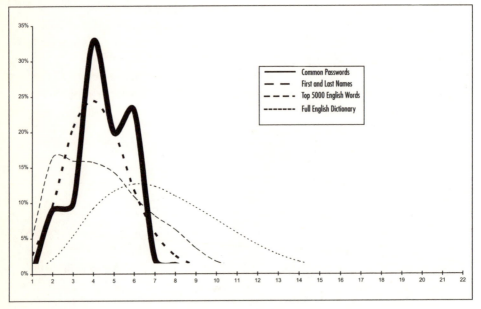

Most techniques for gathering passwords focus on going after the low-hanging fruit—trying common passwords that are six to eight characters in length. Using passwords beyond that length automatically excludes you from many attacks. For example, attackers sometimes use Rainbow Tables, as explained in Chapter 2, to precalculate hashes in order to speed up password-cracking attacks. However, at this time there are no publicly available rainbow tables that go beyond eight characters in length. Using long passwords automatically protects you from rainbow table attacks.

Another real benefit is that in Windows, if you use a password that's 15 characters or longer, Windows does not store the LanMan hash. LanMan hashes are bad because they are particularly vulnerable to some types of password attacks (see Chapter 2 for more on LanMan hashes). If your password is 15 characters or longer, there is no LanMan hash for hackers to go after.

Building Longer Passwords

My own password strategy is to first build a long password, and then make it just a little longer.

However, sometimes the hardest part of building long passwords is coming up with creative techniques to make your passwords longer without making them any harder to remember. The following sections explore some techniques that might help.

Adding Another Word

The simplest way to make your password longer is to add another word along with some kind of punctuation. This can add six to eight characters to the length of your password but only requires remembering one or more pieces of information. Consider, for example, how adding a single word enhances the length of the passwords shown in Table 5.2.

Table 5.2 Adding a Word to Your Password

Before	After
Marty29 (seven characters)	Marty29-thumbnail (17 characters)
Shopping (eight characters)	Goin' shopping (14 characters)
4Chewbacca (ten characters)	4Chewbacca—chewy (16 characters)
Broncos (seven characters)	Broncos helmet. (15 characters)

Bracketing

Bracketing is a technique where you wrap your password in one or more symbols. These symbols could be parentheses, quotes, braces, or just about anything you want. Bracketing only adds a couple more characters to your password, but remember, your strategy should be to make your password longer, and then make it a bit longer. Bracketing is a great way to add that last little bit.

Some examples of bracketing are shown in Table 5.3.

Table 5.3 Bracketing Your Password

Before	After
Starfleet (nine characters)	*Starfleet* (11 characters)
Sugarless (nine characters)	"sugarless" (11 characters)
buyingmoretime (14 characters)	buying(more)time (16 characters)
jamesjames (ten characters)	<<jamesjames>> (14 characters)
Dawghouse (nine characters)	<!—dawghouse—> (14 characters)

Number Patterns

Normally, I would say that adding one or two numbers to the end of your password is not a great strategy, because it is so predictably common. However, adding a long, formatted number somewhere in a password is very effective in increasing both the length and the character diversity of your password. It is okay to use simple patterns in this case because the password as a whole will still be unpredictable.

Some examples of number patterns in passwords are shown in Table 5.4.

Table 5.4 Adding Number Patterns to Your Password

Before	After
Dolphins (eight characters)	Dolphins #919 (13 characters)
JudgeJudy (nine characters)	JudgeJudy 4:00pm (16 characters)
sphYnx (six characters)	$4.99 sphYnx (12 characters)
terriers (eight characters)	93033 terriers (14 characters)

Fun Words

Some words are just more fun to speak or type than others. Consider, for example, the words *guacamole, fandango, chimichanga, zygomatic,* or *vociferous,* which are just more interesting than other words. Take advantage of this and try incorporating these words into your passwords. Other words are interesting for other reasons. For example, the word *lollipop* has just four letters and they all sit next to each other on an English keyboard.

The following is a small collection of words that are just plain fun to say: Ampersand, Bamboozle, Bangkok, Barf, Bongo, Booger, Brouhaha, Buttafuco, Buttock, Canonicalization, Cantankerous, Chimichanga, Circumlocution, Conundrum, Crustacean, Dag Nabbit, Flabbergasted, Flabbergasting, Flatulate, Floccinaucinihilipilification, Gibberish, Glockenspiel, Gobbledygook, Goulash, Hasselhoff, Hobgoblin, Idiosyncratic, Jambalaya, Juxtaposition, Kumquat, Loquacious, Lumpsucker, Mesopotamia, Nugget, Obfuscate, Oligopoly, Orangutan, Oscillate, Phlegm, Platypus, Plethora, Poo Poo Platter, Rancho Cucamonga, Ridiculous, Sassafras, Shenanigans, Spatula, Specificity, Stromboli, Supercalifragilisticexpialidocious, Supercilious, Superfluous, Titicaca, Tomfoolery, Turd, Vehement, Vehicular, Yadda Yadda, Zamboni, Zimbabwe, Zoology.

Repetition

If you have trouble coming up with long passwords, try incorporating repeating patterns. Repetition means that you just remember one piece of information and enter it two or three times. Repeating patterns are tricky because they're somewhat common and predictable. Some password cracking programs, for example, can take a standard dictionary and try repeating each word twice, and can try all those potential passwords in a matter of seconds.

But if your password is already strong on its own, you can bet that repeating it will make it much stronger, without requiring that you remember any additional information. If you slightly modify how you use repetition and incorporate different delimiters, you can further increase the password strength.

The following are some examples of effectively using repetition:

- whiteyogurt-yogurtwhite
- 21bear22bear23
- Pirate—PirateBoat
- tennis/friend/tennis
- 44-forty-four-44
- heads-shoulders-knees-toes-knees-toes
- piano..girl..piano..girl

Prefixes and Suffixes

Adding prefixes and suffixes to regular words not only lengthens your password, it further ensures that your password is unique and will not appear on any common wordlist.

Prefixes and suffixes can be extremely effective with a little creativity:

- non-davincitized
- semi-tigerishly
- off-whitenessless
- pizzatized-sauce
- spicily-peppering

Colorizing

Sometimes when you're really stumped about how to enhance your password, try adding a little color. However, use these type of passwords cautiously because there really aren't that many basic colors to choose from. Nevertheless, they're an easy way to strengthen your password:

- greenish**sheeps
- alice+blue+bulldog
- Yellowing yellow roman
- Strawberry-blue-2
- Dark blue tornadoes

Sentences

Pass phrases have long been a good password strategy. Taking a simple word and turning it into a sentence gives you a chance to not only increase the length of your password but also incorporate punctuation and other symbols:

- Turn left, then turn right, ok?
- Buying 22 more bananas.
- Hiking up Mt. Maple
- It costs $3 more.

Summary

If you want your password to be stronger, make it longer. Think 15 characters or more as a good baseline. But, for those passwords that will protect extra-sensitive information, consider a password of 30 characters or more. Once you get comfortable with techniques like those covered in this chapter, you'll find that your longer passwords are easier to remember, easier to type, and much more difficult to crack. It's not that difficult, it can be fun, and even a child can do it.

Chapter 6

Time: The Enemy of All Secrets

Solutions in this chapter:

- **Aging Passwords**

Aging Passwords

Passwords are secrets and your best passwords should be your best-kept secrets. Nevertheless, passwords age and old secrets are poor secrets. Eventually, your password will expire. The system that handles your password may or may not force you to change an expired password; however, as with all expired items, you should discard it.

It's About Time

Some people say "time is money." Some say that "time flies." Some have "time on their hands" and others have "time to kill." However, time and passwords do not mix. Time is one aspect of password security that you cannot control; you cannot let your passwords get too old.

The primary reason you should regularly change passwords is because password cracking takes time and as time passes the risk of a password being cracked increases. There may be no one trying to crack your password, but you should take precautions based on the assumption that someone is. We do not expect to get in a car accident every time we drive, but we put our seat-belts on every time based on that assumption.

If a password were strong enough that it would take 60 days to crack, then after 60 days the chance of that password being compromised would increase. Every day that passes further increases the risk. Passwords are typed on keyboards, saved on disks, stored in memory, traverse networks, and are sometimes shared with others. All of these things potentially reduce the security of your password over time, and the only way to renew that security is to set a new password.

There are other risks with old passwords. People tend to become attached to passwords and use the same one on multiple systems. Having old passwords that are on multiple systems is dangerous. Regularly changing passwords is a good routine.

Overbearing Policies

Perhaps the most annoying of all password policies is *password aging*. Everyone hates the "Password Expired" message that pops up, especially when rushing to meet a big deadline or otherwise distracted. Moreover, all of the warnings do not really help.

Password policies enforced on computer systems have one primary objective: to prevent people from being careless with their passwords. However, people find ways around policies, so administrators design other policies to prevent people from bypassing the first policies.

Understanding the logic behind the policies can help you understand the need for these policies. Moreover, if you are an administrator who sets these policies, maybe you can adjust these policies to better accommodate your users.

Password Expiration

As mentioned earlier, password expiration is based on the assumption that someone is trying to obtain your password. This may or may not be true, but the fact is that there are many people trying to get many passwords and you do not want your password to be one of them.

Passwords expire because they cannot be protected 100 percent. Hackers have many tools at their disposal to collect passwords and password hashes. You may be the actual target or you may have just been an innocent bystander in another attack. There might be some people at your organization learning to become hackers, so they test out their skills on fellow employees. A system administrator might run the very same tools that hackers use to check the strength of passwords on the system. Your system might be infected with a worm or virus that installed a keylogger. There are thousands of ways your password could be compromised.

The only way to really combat this is to try to stay one step ahead of the hackers and keep changing your passwords. If someone already has your password, hopefully changing it will lock him or her out.

The optimal time to change your password depends on how strong your password is, how important the information that you protect with the password is, and how well protected the system that stores it is. We all have a number of passwords, protecting everything from our sensitive financial accounts to our online shopping carts. A compromise of some accounts would potentially be devastating, while losing a password on another account might be of no consequence. If you want to protect an account, use a strong password and change that password regularly. Some accounts can be left for a year without changing the password, but other passwords should be changed every three months.

Most administrators require users to change their passwords every 60 to 120 days, largely because most people have poor passwords. It turns out that even 60 days is not enough to protect a weak password, so this policy is not quite as effective as it seems. Most weak passwords can be cracked within 24 hours; therefore, 60 days provides little protection. Personally, I would rather choose a very strong password and not have to change it for 120 to 180 days. Any password, no matter how strong it is, eventually expires, but a strong password will last much longer than a weak one.

Creating a password aging policy is tricky. The first priority should be building strong passwords.

Password Histories

Password aging is an important policy, but as soon as administrators started enforcing this policy, users found ways to circumvent it. They would simply alternate between two passwords, switching back and forth every time they were forced to change their passwords. Another trick was to change their password then turn around and change it right back.

This obviously defeats the purpose of requiring a password change. To combat this, administrators found a mechanism called a *password history* to prevent reusing the same passwords repeatedly. A password history is a list of previous passwords that the system uses to prevent you from using the same passwords over again. Some systems keep track of the last few passwords and other systems keep track of more than 20 passwords.

Minimum Age

Everyone thought that was the solution but it did not take long for users to figure out that all they had to do was change their password enough times and then they could flush the list and go back to their original password. So rather than just come up with a better password, they would go through the effort to reset their password a dozen times just to get back to their original passwords. And administrators, rather than teaching people how to build strong passwords, countered with a minimum password age. In other words, after changing a password you had to wait a day before changing it again.

Did Administrators Win?

Now, users have to change their passwords regularly, they cannot reuse them, and they cannot flush their password histories. So are passwords any stronger? No. These policy restrictions have led users to write down their passwords every time they change them, and use predictable patterns such as incrementing a two-digit number after the password. In some ways, their passwords are even less secure.

We all need to step back and remember the original problem, that users normally do not have great passwords. If we all had great passwords, password-aging policies would not be as important. Wouldn't it be great to only have to change your password once or twice a year?

Chapter 7

Living with Passwords

Solutions in this chapter:

- **Making Passwords Convenient**

Making Passwords Convenient

Let's face it; passwords aren't going away anytime soon. Because no matter how much the world's authentication technology advances, chances are it will in some way always depend on a secret that only you know. Meanwhile, password-cracking methodologies will advance, and computers will become increasingly more powerful. You really won't be able to get away with your *cupcake55* or *beachbum* passwords for much longer. You need to learn how to build strong passwords that you can conveniently live with. By convenience, I mean a password that you can easily remember and type easily and quickly.

Remembering Passwords

When my youngest son was five years old, he had a 15-character password for our computer. He had to because that was my policy—even on my home network. Sure, that seems rather extreme for a home network, but I am a security consultant, so it is my job to keep up with the best security practices, even if it is at home. I am not worried about anyone cracking my son's password; it's just my policy, and everyone follows it. My family may hate it, but they follow it.

My son remembered his password just fine and had no trouble typing it in to the computer. What was his password? It was the letter *O* typed 15 times. He happened to like the letter *O,* and he could count to 15 so that was his password. The point is that he found a password that met my policy requirements yet it was something even he could remember. This is what can make passwords so easy to remember: we can build them based on our own experience. We remember the passwords that mean something to us.

Psychologists, scientists, educators, and others have developed many techniques for improving our ability to memorize information. We have all learned techniques such as mnemonics and association. All these techniques are based on the assumption that we are memorizing information that we did not choose. The advantage of memorizing passwords is that you get to choose what you are memorizing. So rather than worrying about how to memorize the passwords you select, you just have to select passwords that you can already memorize.

Several years ago, I set out to create Pafwert, a software application that would randomly generate strong passwords that are easy to remember. The biggest challenge was trying to find out what types of passwords people found most memorable. I based many of my original attempts on well-known memorization techniques, but it turned out that these were not the most effective.

As humans we have different parts of the brain that are tuned for certain tasks. When we memorize something, we may use different parts of our brains. For example, a visual memory, such as remembering someone's face, may be handled by one part of the brain, whereas a memory of a process, such as driving a vehicle, is handled in a completely different manner. The information we remember might contain images, colors, shapes, sounds, smells, tastes, touch, positions, emotions, meaning, knowledge, context, time, and elements of language. The words in a password have some meaning to us, and the letters and characters may form some pattern. The words in a password make a certain sound as we say them in our heads, and typing the password is a kinesthetic process.

I found that the most memorable passwords were those that spread out the work across our brain, making use of various memorization techniques. This combination of techniques makes the password meaningful to us, and therefore, it is easy to remember.

We see this happen all the time with songs. We get some phrase of a song stuck in our heads while we cannot seem to remember other parts of the song (in which case we make up our own words or use the words *blah blah blah* in place of the real words). Why do some parts of the song stick in our heads, while other parts don't? Moreover, why do the most annoying songs seem to be the only ones that become stuck in our heads? That might actually be part of the answer—the fact that a song annoys us might give it meaning for us and therefore make it easier for us to remember.

In the following sections, we discuss some elements that you can use to make your passwords easier to remember.

Rhyming

Do you know what year Columbus sailed the ocean blue? If you know that answer, you probably know it because of a rhyme. Rhyming is a wonderful device that makes a password much easier to remember. Our minds seem to grasp rhymes in such a way that we instantly remember them with little or no effort. An entire phrase becomes a single piece of information in our minds that sometimes has a poetic or musical quality.

To show how much of a difference rhyming makes, consider the rhyming English spelling rule *I before E except after C*. This is a simple rule that English-speaking children learn at a very young age. What makes the rule so simple is that it rhymes. If the rule were *I before R except after H*, it would have nowhere near the rhythmic echo as the real rule.

Here are some examples of passwords that use rhymes:

- Poor-white-dog-bite
- Icecream2extreme
- Teary/weary chicken theory
- Thick, thick Rick

Repetition

Like rhyming, repetition adds a sort of rhythmic echo to our passwords that our minds can easily recall. When used correctly, repetition can create tempo and rhythm in our passwords, thereby making them very easy to remember. And most important, repeating means your password is longer, but there's nothing new to memorize. Remember to integrate repetition into sounds, meanings, and other aspects of your password.

Here are some examples of repetition:

- Chicky-chicky running
- 2bitter@2bitter.com
- C:\files\myfiles\newfiles\
- Purple, purple pineapple

Visualization

Visualization can be a fun device for remembering passwords. We all use visual memories to a varying degree, but it is so much easier to remember a password that we can see in our mind. It doesn't have to be a single image; it can also be a journey or a process that we visualize. The more senses we involve, the easier it will be for us to remember. Here are some examples:

- Jabba the Hut doing the Cha-Cha
- Paquito sat on the apple!
- Frozen banana in my shoe

- Bun–mustard–hot dog–pickles
- Popping packing poppers

Association

It is sometimes intriguing how our minds wander from one thought to another, each thought triggered by an association from a previous thought. After a few minutes of our minds wandering, we marvel how we went from thinking about key lime pie to thinking about a mistake we made on our 1999 tax return. Our minds build complex and often nonsensical associations that trigger our memories. The interesting thing is that the association does not have to be a logical relationship. For example, we can remember a dentist appointment by tying a string around our finger. We see the string and remember our appointment through association (see Figure 7.1).

Figure 7.1 Tying a String on Your Finger As a Reminder

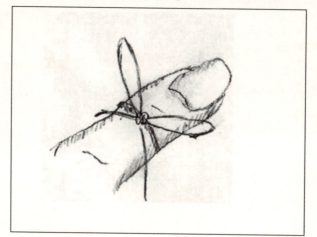

Several years ago, I was traveling for work and purchased a new notebook computer. That night I sat in my hotel room, installed Windows, and set a very strong administrator password. I then created a power user account that I could use daily. While traveling again about a year later, I happened to be in that very same city and at the very same hotel. I had a problem with my laptop and needed to log in to the administrator account to fix it.

I then realized that I had not used that password the entire year and could not remember what I had set. I did not have that password recorded and faced a big problem. I stared around the room contemplating possible solutions. I looked at the furniture. I looked at the coffee pot on the desk. I looked at the curtains. Suddenly, I remembered my password that I had not used in about a year.

How did I remember it? I was sitting in that very same hotel staring at the same furniture, the same coffee pot, and the same curtains when I first set the password. Being back in that environment was enough for my mind to associate these items with my long-forgotten password.

Sure, it might help if your associations are related to the password itself, but this story shows how powerful mental associations can be.

Humor and Irony

If you are one of those people who can never remember a joke, this technique is probably not for you. Nevertheless, we remember things that stand out for us. And funny stuff stands out. Any amount of humor and irony will help you remember your passwords:

- Was Jimi Hendrix's modem a purple Hayes?

- Gone crazy…be back in 5 minutes.

- Your password is unique—like everyone else's we put the "K" in "Kwality."

- Had a handle on security… but it broke.

- A dyslexic man walks into a bra...

- A fish with no eyes is a f sh.

- My reality check just bounced.

Chunking

Chunking has been used for a long time as a memory technique to help people remember things such as phone numbers. A simple fact is that remembering two or three small chunks of information is easier than recalling one large chunk. Research has shown that humans have the capacity to memorize five to nine items at a time. However, we can bypass this limitation by splitting things into smaller chunks and memorizing the chunks.

Here are some ways to use chunking in your passwords:

- Xzr--FFF--8888
- GgggH123-->software
- C51..D45..R22
- Explor+ation+vaca+tion

Exaggeration

Exaggeration is a fun technique that I sometimes use to make memorable passwords. Exaggeration is the technique of extending visual images or facts beyond their expected physical or logical bounds. Here are some examples:

- 43 o'clock
- December 322, 2005
- I Kicked the back of my neck

Offensiveness

Offensive words certainly do stand out. And they will stand out in your minds if you use them in your passwords. Offensive words includes swear words, gross words, slang, racial and religious slurs, crude behaviors, putdowns, insults, alternate words for sexual organs, and so on. If it offends you, or you know it will offend someone else, chances are you will remember it. Here are some examples (Warning: some might be offended).

- brutus@wrinkly-penis.gov
- OK well, just use your imagination…

Gripes

Finally, if something really bugs you, use that for a password:

- It says 10 items or fewer!
- Why is it so hard for you to merge?
- Honk if you ARE Jesus
- Justfindanotherparkingspottheyaren'tgoingtopulloutyoulasyslob

Other Memorization Tips

Despite all these techniques, remembering complex passwords still requires some mental activity. Never try to remember a password in a rush or while you are distracted with other concerns. Don't set a new password right before a weekend or holiday. Relax and think about your password for a few minutes and process it into your mind. Try teaching yourself your password or explaining to yourself the steps you followed to remember the password.

Typing Passwords

When you build a password, you should also consider how you type the password. Before setting a password, I give it a trial run on the keyboard. Some passwords are just harder to type and some passwords are prone to typing mistakes. If your password doesn't flow on the keyboard, just pick something else. Watch out for passwords that force you to type slowly or make obvious movements such as holding down shift to type a punctuation symbol or moving your hand to the number pad to type a long sequence of numbers.

Another thing to consider is how your password sounds when you type it. You can easily tell when someone's password is the same as their username because you hear the same exact typing sounds twice in a row. Some keys, such as the spacebar, make a distinct sound when pressed. Sometimes keyboard sequences, such as QWERTY have a distinct sound to them once you train yourself to hear it. The way a password sounds obviously isn't a huge risk for most people, but it certainly is something to think about.

> **NOTE**
>
> Researchers at the University of California at Berkeley recently showed that using a cheap microphone and widely available software, they could guess passwords just by hearing you type your password. By analyzing unique key click sounds, coupled with their knowledge of the English language, they could achieve accuracy as high as 90 percent.

Key Loggers

Perhaps the greatest risk to password security is a key logger. A key logger is a piece of software or hardware that captures every keystroke that you type. The problem is that no matter how strong your password is, it is completely vulnerable to a key logger attack. For a long time, law enforcement and other government agencies have used key loggers as a form of wiretap, but they are growing in popularity among crackers, and some viruses and worms now even install key loggers to look for passwords and private account numbers.

Anti-keylogger technology has improved lately and is available in an increasing number of products. These applications not only look for tracks left by specific key loggers, but also watch for suspicious behavior common among all key loggers.

Another threat that is much more difficult to detect is a hardware-based key logger. This device plugs in between your keyboard and your computer. These devices are very difficult to detect once installed, but fortunately, someone must have physical access to your computer to install the device. For sensitive systems such as government computers, physical security is the best defense against hardware key loggers.

Most users likely won't ever encounter a hardware key logger attached to their computers, but if you do actually discover one, you probably have much more to worry about than someone just discovering your password.

Managing Passwords

Although I have stressed the importance of remembering passwords, it probably isn't a good idea to rely on your memory alone, especially for accounts that you use infrequently. You should memorize your passwords, but it is prudent to keep a record of the passwords you use. Let's face it; there are just too many passwords you have to remember, and even I record most of my passwords. We are constantly told not to write down our passwords, but that just means don't write them on a sticky note attached to your monitor (see Figure 7.2). And don't try to be clever by attaching it under your keyboard, phone, tissue box, or under your desk. Those have all been done and no matter how clever you think you are, you probably aren't.

Figure 7.2 Don't Stick Passwords on Your Monitor

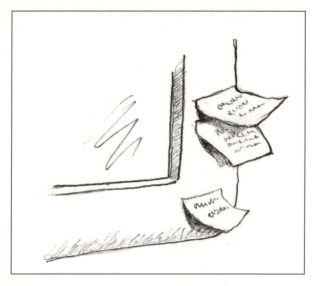

The Difference Is Obscurity

Writing your password down on a sticky note is a bad idea, but recording it in a safe location is a good idea. The difference is obscurity. Security through obscurity is weak security. Obscurity is relying on hiding something as your only means of defense. Real security uses time-tested security practices to ensure that something is safe.

A good example is how many people conceal spare keys to their houses that they can use in emergencies. As cliché as it sounds, many people still put spare keys under their doormats. Placing a key under a potted plant nearby isn't much better. Once someone discovers your hiding place, all security is lost. Therefore, security through obscurity is widely considered a weak form of security.

In contrast, the opposite of this is how a realtor might place a house key in a lock box attached to your doorknob. Anyone with the box's combination can obtain the key to open the door. This allows various realtors to show the house without having to copy and pass around keys. The combination on the lock box is an example of reliable security.

TIP

Security through obscurity is weak, but obscurity can be useful as an additional layer on top of legitimate security methods. In the lock box example, this would mean keeping the key in a lock box and then hiding the lock box. Someone would have to locate the box, but once he or she found it, that person would still have to deal with the combination.

Password management software is like a lock box. These software applications securely store your sensitive data by encrypting it with a strong master password. You can record all your passwords, but to retrieve them, you have to remember only the master password. Of course, you do have to memorize that master password, and it should be one of your strongest passwords. You protect all your passwords with one big strong password.

If you think about it, a password really is a form of obscurity. A password is a secret that compromises all security if someone else discovers it. The distinction between a password and the location of a house key is that passwords, hopefully, are not easy to discover and therefore are a strong secret. It is easier to search around a house for a key than to search a keyspace with trillions of combinations. Strong passwords allow for so many possible combinations that they are considered strong security. Therefore, using a password manager is not security through obscurity.

So many password managers are available that it is hard to recommend a specific one. If you visit software Web sites such as www.tucows.com/downloads/Windows/Security/GeneralSecurity/PasswordManagers/ you can search through catalogs of these software applications to find one that best suits your needs. Make sure you feel comfortable using the application; otherwise, you won't use it.

There are alternatives to these tools that might work better in some situations. I personally prefer the flexibility of an Excel spreadsheet. But if you use

Excel, be sure to protect it with a password. You can do this when you save the document (see Figure 7.3).

Figure 7.3 Adding Password Protection to an Excel File

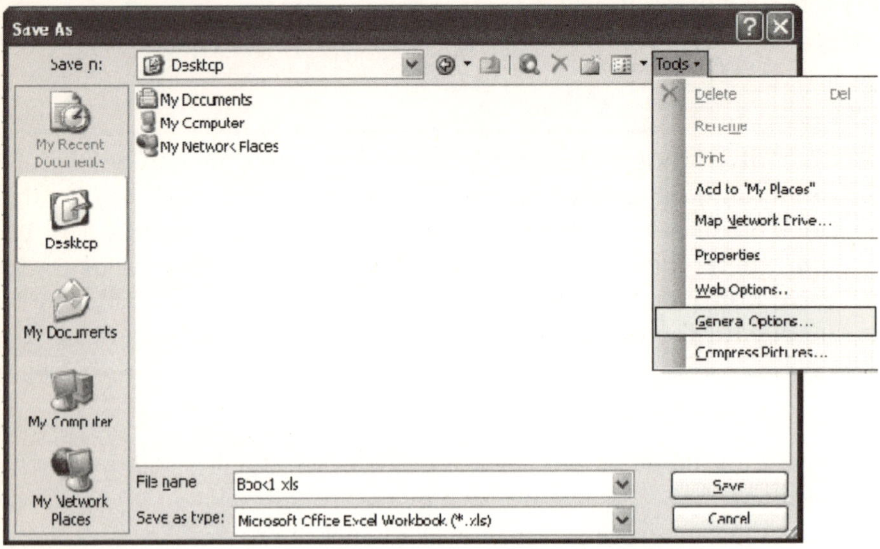

From there, set a Password to open and click on the **Advanced** button to select more encryption options (see Figure 7.4).

Figure 7.4 Encryption Options

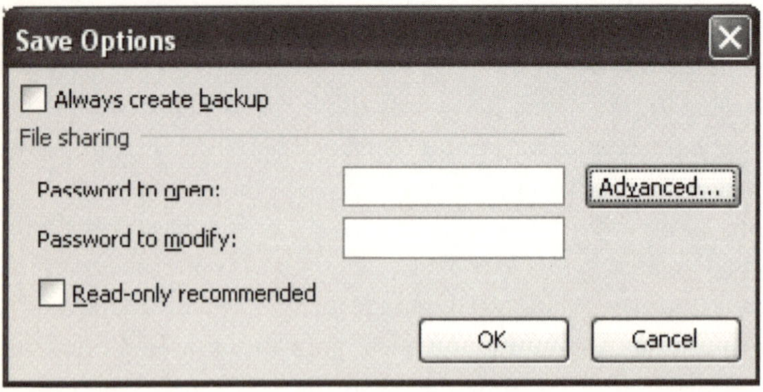

Never use "Weak Encryption (XOR)" or "Office 97/2000-Compatible" encryption because they provide little protection, and both can be broken in just a few minutes or less. They are somewhat similar to the tiny locks some people place on their luggage. Choose the Microsoft Strong Cryptographic Provider with a key length of 128 bits (the maximum allowed), as shown in Figure 7.5.

Figure 7.5 Encryption Types

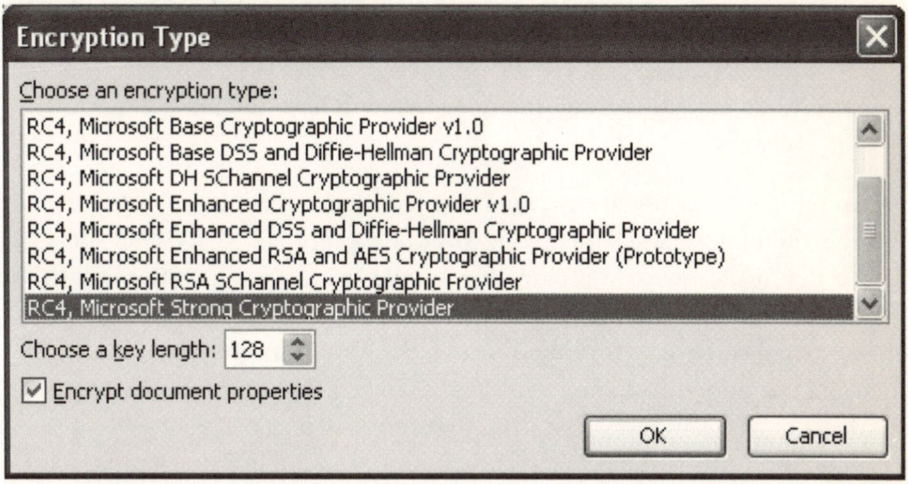

Besides password protecting the file, it would also help to give it an obscure name. At least don't name it passwords.xls. You should also store the file in a secure location that has limited access. Another alternative is to store the file on a portable USB drive that you can take with you.

Secret Questions

To help verify a user's identity in the case of a lost password, many applications use secret questions. By answering a preselected question, a user can demonstrate some personal knowledge, thereby proving account ownership. A classic example is asking to provide a mother's maiden name.

To guess a secret question, an attacker would likely have to know something about the user, but secret questions break all the rules for strong passwords and have some significant weaknesses:

- An attacker can often discover the information with casual research.

- The answer to the question is usually a fact that will never change.

- Users reuse the same secret questions and answers across multiple Web sites.

- Someone close to the individual may know the answer to many of the questions.

- People rarely, if ever, change their secret questions.

- The answers are often case-insensitive and usually contain a limited character set.

- Some questions have a limited number of answers.

- With some questions, many people will have the same common answers.

Secret questions usually ask for some fact that hopefully only the account owner would know, and supposedly would never forget. Many Web sites assume that if the user can provide the answer to the question, this is sufficient to identify the user. However, many secret questions ask for facts that anyone could discover with little research. To make things worse, if someone discovers this information you can't just change a fact from the past.

Because of this weakness, it is important to understand that secret questions are not a strong means of authentication, and applications should use them only to initiate a password change request via e-mail or some other mechanism. This prevents anonymous attacks on the password reset process. Providing the answer to a secret question should never be enough to validate a user, but when combined with other factors, such as having access to the user's e-mail account, these answers can be effective in helping to identify a user. If you ever see a Web site or some application let you log in to your account with a secret question alone, do us all a favor and drop them an e-mail complaining about this risk.

I have also seen countless Web sites that provide great tips on avoiding easily guessable passwords, but then turn around and ask for a dog's name or what city you were born in to answer a secret question. Some secret questions are so easily guessable that they are absurd as a form of security.

Even if an attacker knows nothing about the target user, the nature of secret questions limits the possible range of answers. For example, consider the questions and ranges of answers shown in Table 7.1. As the table shows, many secret questions have so few possible answers that a brute-force attack against these secret questions is completely feasible. To make matters worse, some Web sites fail to detect or prevent brute-force attacks against secret questions. Security experts for years have told people to avoid using pet names, family names, or dates in passwords, but secret questions go directly against that advice.

Table 7.1 Secret Questions and Ranges of Answers

Question	Range of Answers
What is the name of your favorite pet?	The top 20 dog names are Max, Buddy, Molly, Bailey, Maggie, Lucy, Jake, Rocky, Sadie, Lucky, Daisy, Jack, Sam, Shadow, Bear, Buster, Lady, Ginger, Abby, and Toby.
In what city were you born?	The top 10 largest U.S. cities are New York, Los Angeles, Chicago, Houston, Philadelphia, Phoenix, San Diego, Dallas, San Antonio, and Detroit; one in three of all U.S. citizens live in the top 250 cities; the top 10 most common U.S. city names are Fairview, Midway, Oak Grove, Franklin, Riverside, Centerville, Mount Pleasant, Georgetown, Salem, and Greenwood.
What high school did you attend?	There are approximately 25,000 to 30,000 high schools in the U.S.; you can use classmates.com to get a list by U.S. state and city.
What is your favorite movie?	For a list of the all-time top 250 films, see www.imdb.com/top_250_films
What is your mother's maiden name?	There are approximately 25,000 common surnames; 1 in 10 U.S. citizens have the surname Smith, Johnson, Williams, Jones, Brown, Davis, Miller, Wilson, Moore, Taylor, Anderson, Thomas, Jackson, White, Harris, Martin, Thompson, Garcia, Martinez, Robinson, Clark, Rodriguez, Lewis, Lee, Walker, Hall, Allen, or Young.
What street did you grow up on?	The 10 most common street names are Second/2nd, Third/3rd, First/1st, Fourth/4th, Park, Fifth/5th, Main, Sixth/6th, Oak, Seventh/7th, Pine, Maple, Cedar, Eighth/8th, and Elm.

Continued

Table 7.1 continued Secret Questions and Ranges of Answers

Question	Range of Answers
What was the make of your first car?	Most cars are built by Acura, Audi, BMW, Buick, Cadillac, Chevrolet, Chrysler, Daewoo, Dodge, Ford, GMC, Honda, Hummer, Hyundai, Infiniti, Isuzu, Jaguar, Jeep, Kia, Land Rover, Lexus, Lincoln, Mazda, Mercedes-Benz, Mercury, Mitsubishi, Nissan, Oldsmobile, Plymouth, Pontiac, Porsche, Saab, Saturn, Subaru, Suzuki, Toyota, Volkswagen, and Volvo.
What is your anniversary?	The average length of a marriage is 7.2 years, giving 2,628 likely dates.
What is your favorite color?	There are around 100 common colors, even considering colors such as taupe, gainsboro, and fuschia.

The greatest threat with secret questions is that the answer is usually fixed, and an attacker can sometimes discover this information through research. Because there are usually a limited set of answers to secret questions, they are also vulnerable to brute-force attacks. Finally, secret questions are usually ineffective against attacks by those close to the user. Individuals such as ex-spouses, once-close business associates, or wayward teenage children may have sufficient information and sufficient motivation to break into a user's account. Once someone knows you, there is little you can do to protect yourself. It's not as if you can go and change your mother's maiden name.

When you set a secret question and answer pair, use caution to pick a strong question that has many possible answers. It might even be helpful to add a small secret code, such as a three-digit number and letter combination (see Appendix B). You can probably reuse that code on all your secret questions. It won't completely protect you but it will limit your exposure to certain types of attacks.

Sometimes an application will let you set your own secret question. If that is the case, watch out for common mistakes that people make. I often see secret questions that provide little security or make little sense. Here are examples of poor secret questions:

- What year were you born?

- What is your password?

- What is the capital of Georgia?

Select good questions, carefully considering the possible range of answers, as well as the likelihood of common answers. Use unique questions and try to avoid subjects that return short, one-word answers. Also try to avoid questions that others commonly use, such as mother's maiden name, pet name, or high school. But keep in mind that you should ask questions that users will always answer the same.

Here are some examples of good secret questions:

- What is the first and last name of your first boyfriend or girlfriend?

- Which phone number do you remember most from your childhood?

- What was your favorite place to visit as a child?

- Who was your favorite actor, musician, or artist when you were 16?

Summary

Remembering passwords can be easy if you build passwords that you already know you can remember. Our brains are terrible at processing random, unrelated pieces of information, but if we throw in a few techniques such as rhyming and association, we can develop passwords that we instantly remember.

Chapter 8

Ten Password Pointers: Building Strong Passwords

Solutions in this chapter:

- **Building Strong Passwords**

Introduction

Sometimes coming up with a good password can be difficult. When faced with choosing a password, many people seem to get some kind of tunnel vision and they suddenly cannot see beyond their own desk. At that point, all that comes to mind is a dog's name, a football team, or an item within immediate view. Most often, people simply use one of their favorite passwords—the ones they always use.

Building Strong Passwords

The secret to strong passwords is to not *choose* a password, but to *build* a password. Don't just think of some word and use that as your password. Use some specific technique to construct a complex password that is not only effective but easy to remember. Here are some of my favorite tips for building strong passwords that you yourself can use those times when you get stumped for ideas.

WARNING

I shouldn't have to say this, but unfortunately it must be said: please don't use any of the password examples you see in this book or any place else as your actual password. They are simply examples. In fact, you are best off not even using these exact passwords patterns, but to instead be creative and use them as models for your own ideas.

Three Words

A simple technique for increasing the strength of your password is to just use more than one word. Some people would call this a *pass phrase*, but this particular technique is somewhat different. The difference is that you select three or more words that are not necessarily grammatically related, but have something else in common.

The technique revolves around picking three words that are related enough for you to easily remember them, but if others knew one of the words, they couldn't easily guess the other words.

For example, you could pick three synonyms, three homonyms, three antonyms, three words that rhyme, or three words that have the same prefix. The key here is to provide enough randomness that your password is not predictable. Try to throw in numbers, capitals, punctuation, or other variants to make your password even stronger.

The following are some examples:

- 33 free trees
- Walking, talking, keyring
- Little-ladle-lady
- ChalkingChangeRange

Our minds remember bits, or chunks of information. This pattern lets you easily create passwords of 20 or more characters. Despite that, all your brain has to do is remember a few bits of information—the three words you selected.

The key to this particular technique is to have one common element in each word to help you remember the password and to assist you in thinking of unique words beyond things personal or in your environment. By choosing words related to each other in different ways, it forces you to be more creative. There are many ways to connect words beyond meaning alone.

Did You Know?

You have probably heard of synonyms and antonyms, but have you heard of an oronym? Here is a list of various nym words and their meanings:

- **Ambigram** A word or words that can be read in more than one direction, such as rotated or reflected (SWIMS, MOM).
- **Anagram** Letters from one word rearranged to form another word (act versus cat).
- **Ananym** A pseudonym made by reversing a name (James versus Semaj).
- **Antagonym** A single word that has conflicting meanings (dust, as in remove dust versus dust, to add dust, as in dusting for fingerprints).
- **Antonym** Two words with opposite or near opposite meanings (up versus down).
- **Autoantonym** Same as an antagonym.

- **Autonym** A word that describes itself (mispelled is misspelled; noun is a noun).
- **Capitonym** A word that changes meaning when capitalized (Polish versus polish).
- **Contranym, Contronym** Same as antagonym.
- **Exonym** A place name that foreigners use instead of the name that locals use (Spain versus Espana).
- **Heteronym** Words that have the same spelling but different meanings or pronunciation (produce, read, convert).
- **Homographs** Same as heteronym.
- **Homonym** Words with the same pronunciation or spelling but different meanings (reign and rain).
- **Homophone** Words that are pronounced the same but spelled differently (flu versus flew).
- **Hypernym** The type of one word in relationship to another (bird is the hypernym of robin; animal is the hypernym of bird).
- **Hyponym** The specific type of one word in relationship to another (robin is a hyponym of bird; cat is the hyponym of animal).
- **Oronym** Similar to a homophone but made up of a series of words (ice cream versus I scream; kiss the sky versus kiss this guy).
- **Pseudoantonym** A word that appears to have a meaning opposite of its actual meaning (inflammable, unloose).
- **Synonyms** Two words that have the same or nearly the same meaning (build and assemble).

The E-Mail Address

People are usually surprised when they see me type in such long passwords and want to know how I remember these. It's simple: society has trained our brains to easily learn certain patterns, so I build passwords to mimic those patterns. These always make great passwords. One of my personal favorites is to pattern a password after a fake e-mail address. It is one of my favorites because it contains so many of the elements of a strong secret.

Here's how it works: first, think of a name of anything, fake or real. Then think of a symbolic, meaningful, funny, or ironic phrase related to that name. Finally, put those together, add a dot-com (or other extension), and you have an e-mail address password. Let me illustrate:

Pick a name:	Dr. Seuss
Choose a related phrase:	Green Eggs
Result:	Dr.Seuss@greeneggs.com

Pick a name:	Kermit
Choose a related phrase:	The Muppets
Result:	Kermit@themuppets.org

Pick a name:	Rover
Choose a related phrase:	Hates cats
Result:	rover22@rover-hates-cats.net

These passwords are effective because we add a couple punctuation symbols and it's easy to increase the length of your passwords without making them any harder to remember. This pattern is particularly flexible and the combinations are endless.

Here are some more examples illustrating variants of this pattern:

- Cat-Lover2005@aol.com
- Your-mama@uglystick.com
- yoda@strong-this-password-is.net
- Ben@dover.org
- e-mailme@home
- me@com.net.org.com

The URL

Similar to the e-mail address password is the URL password. We're constantly bombarded with WWW addresses, so why not take advantage of that and model your passwords after that pattern? Here are some examples:

- www.sendallyourmoney.irs.gov
- www.someone_smells.net
- ftp.droppedout.edu
- www.go.ahead.and.try.to.crack.this.password.com

TIP

There's no reason to stop with just one domain extension or even valid extensions. In the past, I've used extensions such as .com.net.com, .edu.sux, .gov.waste, and so on. The more you divert from the standards, the more opportunity you have to increase the *entropy* of the password, as explained in Chapter 3.

The Title

Sometimes you need to build a password and you're just stuck. No matter what you try, the system seems to reject it, saying that your password does not meet complexity requirements. Here's a simple pattern that should produce passwords that meet the requirements of even the strictest password system. This is how it works:

First, think of a title prefix.

Here's a list to choose from: Admiral, Baron, Brother, Capt., Captain, Chief, Colonel, Commander, Congressman, Count, Countess, Dame, Deacon, Deaconess, Doc, Doctor, Dr, Dr., Farmer, Father, Gen., General, Governor, Judge, Justice, King, Lady, Lieutenant, Lord, Madam, Madame, Mademoiselle, Major, Master, Mayor, Miss, Mister, Monsieur, Monsignor, Mother, Mr., Mrs., Ms., Officer, President, Prince, Princess, Private, Prof., Professor, Queen, Rabbi, Rev., Reverend, Sergeant, Seaman, Secretary, Senator, Sheikh, Sir, or Sister.

Next, think of a first name, male or female, or a surname.

Think of an adjective, something that describes a noun, such as cheerful, red, wet, and so on.

Finally, add a comma, and then an ordinal number, such as 1st, 2nd, 3rd, and so forth.

When you put these elements together, you should end up with passwords like these:

- President Pink, the 2nd

- Dr. Hurt, the 3rd

- Professor Pencil, the 1st

- 1st Lieutenant Lucky

The strength of this password pattern is that it produces long passwords and insures that you use capital letters, numbers, and usually punctuation symbols. Make sure you don't use your own name and this should meet just about any system complexity requirements. If the system still rejects your password, try leaving out the spaces.

In my own experience, the only times I have had this password rejected is when the system says my password is too long!

Number Rhymes

This pattern is another one of my personal favorites, but you need to be careful and creative because there are some limitations on how many unique passwords it will produce.

The pattern is simple: pick a number, preferably more than two digits, and then add on a word or phrase that rhymes with that number. You should end up with passwords like the following:

- 23 Strawberry!

- 209 Canadian Pine!

- Number 8, Armor Plate

- 425 Take a Drive!

- Number Two, Oh Phew!

To help you out with rhyming words we have included some basic rhyme lists in the next few sections of this chapter. Many of these rhyming words can be found at www.rhymezone.com.

The following mini-sections offer some words that rhyme with numbers.

Rhymes with One

Bun, Bunn, Done, Fun, Hun, None, Nun, Pun, Run, Shun, Son, Spun, Stun, Sun, Ton, Tonne, Won, Bank Run, Bon Ton, Bull Run, Cross Bun, Dry Run, End Run, Fowl Run, Gross Ton, Homerun, Home Run, Long Run, Long Ton, Make Fun, Mean Sun, Net Ton, Outdone, Outrun, Pit Run, Redone, Rerun, Short Ton, Ski Run, Undone, Chicken Run, Honey Bun, Hotdog Bun, Hot Cross Bun, Metric Ton, Midnight Sun, Overdone, Caramel Bun, Cinnamon Bun, Favorite Son, Frankfurter Bun, Hamburger Bun, In The Long Run.

Rhymes with Two

Bleu, Blew, Blue, Boo, Brew, Chew, Choo, Clue, Coup, Coups, Crew, Cue, Deux, Dew, Do, Doo, Drew, Ewe, Few, Flew, Flu, Foo, Glue, Gnu, Goo, Grew, Hue, Knew, New, Phew, Rue, Shoe, Shoo, Skew, Slew, Spew, Stew, Threw, Through, Thru, Too, You, And You, Bamboo, Beef Stew, Canoe, Dark Blue, Go Through, Go To, Ground Crew, Gym Shoe, Make Do, Not Due, Ooze Through, Slice Through, Soak Through, Speak To, Squeak Through, Stage Crew, Steel Blue, Thank You, Withdrew, Appeal To, Attach To, Cheese Fondue, Chicken Stew, Cobalt Blue, Grow Into, Hitherto, What Are You, Long-Overdue, Blink 182, Chicken Cordon Bleu, Critical Review, Giant Kangaroo, Outrigger Canoe, With Reference To, Capital Of Peru, Giant Timber Bamboo, Literary Review, Security Review.

Rhymes with Three

At Sea, Banshee, Bay Tree, Beach Flea, Beach Pea, Bead Tree, Bean Tree, Black Pea, Black Sea, Black Tea, Debris, Decree, Deedee, Degree, Dundee, Fig Tree, Herb Tea, High Sea, Abductee, Absentee, Addressee, Christmas Tree, Detainee, Entrance Fee, Escapee, German Bee, Middle C, Third Degree, Vitamin B, Vitamin C, Vitamin D, Vitamin E, Vitamin G, Vitamin P, To The Lowest Degree, Africanized Honey Bee, Battle Of The Bismarck Sea, Capital Of Tennessee, Mediterranean Sea.

Rhymes with Four

Boar, Bore, Chore, Core, Corps, Door, Drawer, For, Fore, Gore, More, Pour, Roar, Wore, Explore, Fall For, Front Door, Lead Ore, No More, Offshore, Price War, Restore, What For, Wild Boar, World War, Account For, Allow For, Anymore, Know The Score, Liquor Store, Sliding Door, Computer Store, Convenience Store, Department Store, Prisoner Of War, Responsible For, Uranium Ore, American Civil War.

Rhymes with Five

Clive, Clyve, Dive, Drive, Hive, I've, Jive, Live, Shive, Strive, Thrive, Alive, Arrive, C5, Connive, Contrive, Crash Dive, Deprive, Derive, Disc Drive, Disk Drive, Hard Drive, Let Drive, Line Drive, M5, Nose Dive, Revive, Survive, Swan Dive, Tape Drive, Test Drive, Backhand Drive, CD Drive, Come Alive, Fluid Drive, Forehand Drive, Power Dive, Take A Dive, External Drive, Internal Drive, Winchester Drive, Automatic Drive.

Rhymes with Six

Bix, Bricks, Brix, Chicks, Clicks, Cliques, Dix, Fickes, Fix, Flicks, Fricks, Frix, Hicks, Hix, Ickes, Kicks, Knicks, Licks, Mix, Nick's, Nicks, Nikk's, Nix, Nyx, Picks, Pix, Rick's, Ricks, Rix, Slicks, Styx, Ticks, Tics, Tricks, Vic's, Vicks, Wickes, Wicks, Wix, Affix, Cake Mix, Conflicts, Depicts, Inflicts, Predicts, Quick Fix, Transfix, Bag Of Tricks, Brownie Mix, Captain Hicks, Intermix, River Styx, Row Of Bricks, Lemonade Mix.

Rhymes with Seven

Bevan, Beven, Devan, Devon, Evan, Evon, Heaven, Kevan, Leaven, Levan, Previn, Eleven, Mcgrevin, Mcnevin, Seventh Heaven, Tree Of Heaven, Vault Of Heaven, Manna From Heaven , Kevin, 7-Eleven, , Momevin, Geven, Deven, Beven, Weven, Pevin, Feven, Geven, Jeven, Zeven, Meven, Breven, Toobeven.

Rhymes with Eight

Ate, Bait, Freightgate, Great, Hate, Late, Mate, Bank Rate, Baud Rate, Clean Slate, Collate, Crime Rate, Debate, Deflate, Dictate, Dilate, Kuwait, Lightweight, Lose Weight, Postdate, Steel Plate, Figure Skate, Mental State, Overrate, Overweight, Payment Rate, Police State, Procreate, Quarter Plate, Real Estate, Recreate, Reinstate, Roller Skate, Running Mate, Underrate,

Watergate, Collection Plate, Junior Lightweight, Prime Interest Rate, Public Debate, Recriminate, Remunerate, Repayment Rate, Reporting Weight, Second Estate, Turnover Rate, Vacancy Rate, Department Of State, Emotional State, Equivalent Weight, Maturity Date, Unemployment Rate, Alexander The Great, Capital Of Kuwait, Secretary Of State.

Rhymes with Nine

Brine, Dine, Fine, Line, Mine, Pine, Shine, Shrine, Twine, Vine, Whine, Wine, Blood Line, Blush Wine, Bread Line, Bus Line, Chalk Line, Chow Line, Combine, Confine, Consign, Hot Line, Incline, Malign, Nut Pine, Plumb Line, Plus Sign, Rail Line, Street Sign, Tree Line, Trend Line, White Pine, Chorus Line, Command Line, Copper Mine, Credit Line, Dollar Sign, Draw A Line, Draw The Line, Drop A Line, Equal Sign, Fishing Line, Melon Vine, Minus Sign, Opening Line, Percentage Sign, Telephone Line, Top Of The Line, Unemployment Line, Personal Credit Line.

Get to the Point

What makes a password predictable is not just the meaning of your password, but also the actual words you use. One way to circumvent this problem is to say something in a roundabout way. For example, rather than using the password *my sister*, put it this way: *my mother's husband's daughter*. Instead of using the password *stapler*, instead use the password *staple contortion device*. Get the point?

Some examples:

- Lap-based computing device
- The circular filing cabinet
- Armpit odor prevention system

A variant of this technique is to take any word, phrase, or job title and make it sound politically correct:

- Waste collection engineer
- Follicle deprived

Yet another variant of this technique is to use a Jeopardy-like style where you use the answer as your password instead of the question. It doesn't really matter what the answer is, you're just using the actual question to make a strong password.

- What is the color of your car?
- Who was the first person to travel to Jupiter?

The Confession

One problem too many people have is sharing their passwords with others. It's just too easy when someone needs something that your password protects, to just hand the password over to them without thinking. Of course, as I explain in Chapter 11, this is not a good practice because a password should be a secret. You should *never* share your passwords with anyone else. So here's a trick to make yourself think twice before blurting out your password: make your password a confession—a real secret.

You could, for example, make your password *I pick my nose at stoplights*. Of course, this is just a made up confession, not something I am really admitting to. That would be disgusting. But suppose you yourself pick your nose at stoplights; this might be a good password for *you*. It certainly will help you keep your password to yourself.

So what secrets do you have? Do you dislike someone? Do you steal office supplies from your company? Wear a toupee? They're all great passwords.

The great thing about this password tip is that these passwords are also easy to remember. Whatever it is that popped into your head first is probably something you're self-conscious enough about to make you think of it first. Best of all, this might just be one of your best kept secrets. What better way to remember a password than by basing it on something that you already keep a secret?

The Elbow Mambo

You may have heard of dance moves called the pot stir, the duck walk, or the egg beater, but here's a chance to come up with your own dance move. Well, at least the name of it. There really isn't much to explain here, but maybe a few examples might get you started:

- The Puppy Hop
- The knee-dip-trip
- The Wild Boar
- The Larry King Shrug

Passwords based on these patterns are simple to remember, and probably easier than the dance moves themselves.

The Phone Number

I already mentioned using patterns our brains are accustomed to remembering. Another technique in this category is a password based on a phone number. When you think of these passwords, be sure to include numbers, punctuation, and letters.

The following are some examples:

- 1-800-Broken glasses
- (888) 888-eight eight
- 1-900-puppies
- (222) New-Shoe

This pattern usually works well; just be careful not to use an easily guessable number such as your own number or some commonly known number. Although, the pattern "(888) 888-eight eight" might seem repetitive and simple, the fact that we utilize spaces, -, ( ), and that it's 22 characters long makes it a difficult password to crack.

NOTE

Approximately 1 out of every 110,000 people uses the password *8675309*, from the 1982 Tommy Tutone hit single *Jenny*.

Letter Swapping

One principle of strong passwords is to avoid using dictionary words as your password. A simple way to avoid doing this is using a couple of words together, separated by a space or hyphen. For years, AOL has used this technique for generating passwords on their mass-mailed free offer CDs. On these CDs, you will frequently see passwords such as *ANTICS-ABSORB*, *HOLE-ROTS*, or *RAKED-GNOME*. The only problem with this technique is that as computing power increases, it would not be difficult for a hacker to try every combination of two words to discover the password. Even current technology makes that feasible.

This password technique is similar to the two-words method. The difference is that it takes it one step further by swapping the first one or two letters of each word to make it less likely they will appear on a dictionary or common password list. These types of words are called spoonerisms.

This is what they look like:

- *Sour Grape* becomes *Gour Srape*

- *Ford Mustang* becomes *Mord Fustang*

- *Slurred Speech* becomes *Spurred Sleech*

- *Dog-Poo* becomes *Pog-Doo*

- *Big Ditch!* becomes *Dig Bitch!*

This pattern might help you to remember your password, given two new elements: humor and offensiveness. If something is funny, it's easier to remember. Same thing goes for offensive words. Sure, you might be offended by the password *Dig Bitch*, but chances are you probably will remember it. The only problem with that particular password is that by swapping letters it made two new words that are still dictionary words, so watch out for that.

Constructing a memorable password is easy if you take the time to learn some simple patterns such as those presented here. If you use these patterns or come up with your own, just be sure you don't make your passwords so similar that someone could guess many of your passwords just by seeing one of them. The goal is to make each and every password unique but still easy to remember.

Summary

By now, you should have a feel for the strategy here—follow patterns that are easy to remember but make your passwords less predictable. Think about building a password, rather than just choosing a password. Complex, multi-word passwords are much more difficult to crack and they can be just as easy to remember as a short password. Best of all, sometimes all you need to remember the password is just one of the words contained in it to trigger remembering the rest.

Chapter 9

The 500 Worst Passwords of All Time

Solutions in this chapter:

- **The Worst Passwords**

The Worst Passwords

From the moment people started using passwords, it didn't take long to realize how many people picked the very same passwords over and over. Even the way people misspell words is consistent. In fact, people are so predictable that most hackers make use of lists of common passwords just like these.

To give you some insight into how predictable humans are, the following is a list of the 500 most common passwords. If you see your password on this list, please change it immediately. Keep in mind that every password listed here has been used by at least hundreds if not thousands of other people.

There are some interesting passwords on this list that show how people try to be clever, but even human cleverness is predictable. For example, look at these passwords that I found interesting:

- **ncc1701** The ship number for the Starship Enterprise

- **thx1138** The name of George Lucas' first movie, a 1971 remake of an earlier student project

- **qazwsx** Follows a simple pattern when typed on a typical keyboard

- **666666** Six sixes

- **7777777** Seven sevens

- **ou812** The title of a 1988 Van Halen album

- **8675309** The number mentioned in the 1982 Tommy Tutone song. The song supposedly caused an epidemic of people dialing 867-5309 and asking for "Jenny."

NOTE

Approximately one out of every nine people uses at least one password on the list shown in Table 9.1! And one out of every 50 people uses one of the top 20 worst passwords.

The Passwords

Table 9.1 lists the top 500 worst passwords of all time, not considering character case. Don't blame me for the offensive words; you were the ones who picked these, not me.

Table 9.1 The Top 500 Worst Passwords of All Time

Top 1-100	Top 101–200	Top 201–300	Top 301–400	Top 401–500
123456	porsche	firebird	prince	rosebud
password	guitar	butter	beach	jaguar
12345678	chelsea	united	amateur	great
1234	black	turtle	7777777	cool
pussy	diamond	steelers	muffin	cooper
12345	nascar	tiffany	redsox	1313
dragon	jackson	zxcvbn	star	scorpio
qwerty	cameron	tomcat	testing	mountain
696969	654321	golf	shannon	madison
mustang	computer	bond007	murphy	987654
letmein	amanda	bear	frank	brazil
baseball	wizard	tiger	hannah	lauren
master	xxxxxxxx	doctor	dave	japan
michael	money	gateway	eagle1	naked
football	phoenix	gators	11111	squirt
shadow	mickey	angel	mother	stars
monkey	bailey	junior	nathan	apple
abc123	knight	thx1138	raiders	alexis
pass	iceman	porno	steve	aaaa
fuckme	tigers	badboy	forever	bonnie
6969	purple	debbie	angela	peaches
jordan	andrea	spider	viper	jasmine
harley	horny	melissa	ou812	kevin
ranger	dakota	booger	jake	matt
iwantu	aaaaaa	1212	lovers	qwertyui

Continued

Table 9.1 continued The Top 500 Worst Passwords of All Time

Top 1-100	Top 101–200	Top 201–300	Top 301–400	Top 401–500
jennifer	player	flyers	suckit	danielle
hunter	sunshine	fish	gregory	beaver
fuck	morgan	porn	buddy	4321
2000	starwars	matrix	whatever	4128
test	boomer	teens	young	runner
batman	cowboys	scooby	nicholas	swimming
trustno1	edward	jason	lucky	dolphin
thomas	charles	walter	helpme	gordon
tigger	girls	cumshot	jackie	casper
robert	booboo	boston	monica	stupid
access	coffee	braves	midnight	shit
love	xxxxxx	yankee	college	saturn
buster	bulldog	lover	baby	gemini
1234567	ncc1701	barney	cunt	apples
soccer	rabbit	victor	brian	august
hockey	peanut	tucker	mark	3333
killer	john	princess	startrek	canada
george	johnny	mercedes	sierra	blazer
sexy	gandalf	5150	leather	cumming
andrew	spanky	doggie	232323	hunting
charlie	winter	zzzzzz	4444	kitty
superman	brandy	gunner	beavis	rainbow
asshole	compaq	horney	bigcock	112233
fuckyou	carlos	bubba	happy	arthur
dallas	tennis	2112	sophie	cream
jessica	james	fred	ladies	calvin
panties	mike	johnson	naughty	shaved
pepper	brandon	xxxxx	giants	surfer
1111	fender	tits	booty	samson
austin	anthony	member	blonde	kelly

Continued

Table 9.1 continued The Top 500 Worst Passwords of All Time

Top 1-100	Top 101–200	Top 201–300	Top 301–400	Top 401–500
william	blowme	boobs	fucked	paul
daniel	ferrari	donald	golden	mine
golfer	cookie	bigdaddy	0	king
summer	chicken	bronco	fire	racing
heather	maverick	penis	sandra	5555
hammer	chicago	voyager	pookie	eagle
yankees	joseph	rangers	packers	hentai
joshua	diablo	birdie	einstein	newyork
maggie	sexsex	trouble	dolphins	little
biteme	hardcore	white	0	redwings
enter	666666	topgun	chevy	smith
ashley	willie	bigtits	winston	sticky
thunder	welcome	bitches	warrior	cocacola
cowboy	chris	green	sammy	animal
silver	panther	super	slut	broncos
richard	yamaha	qazwsx	8675309	private
fucker	justin	magic	zxcvbnm	skippy
orange	banana	lakers	nipples	marvin
merlin	driver	rachel	power	blondes
michelle	marine	slayer	victoria	enjoy
corvette	angels	scott	asdfgh	girl
bigdog	fishing	2222	vagina	apollo
cheese	david	asdf	toyota	parker
matthew	maddog	video	travis	qwert
121212	hooters	london	hotdog	time
patrick	wilson	7777	paris	sydney
martin	butthead	marlboro	rock	women
freedom	dennis	srinivas	xxxx	voodoo
ginger	fucking	internet	extreme	magnum
blowjob	captain	action	redskins	juice

Continued

Table 9.1 continued The Top 500 Worst Passwords of All Time

Top 1-100	Top 101–200	Top 201–300	Top 301–400	Top 401–500
nicole	bigdick	carter	erotic	abgrtyu
sparky	chester	jasper	dirty	777777
yellow	smokey	monster	ford	dreams
camaro	xavier	teresa	freddy	maxwell
secret	steven	jeremy	arsenal	music
dick	viking	11111111	access14	rush2112
falcon	snoopy	bill	wolf	russia
taylor	blue	crystal	nipple	scorpion
111111	eagles	peter	iloveyou	rebecca
131313	winner	pussies	alex	tester
123123	samantha	cock	florida	mistress
bitch	house	beer	eric	phantom
hello	miller	rocket	legend	billy
scooter	flower	theman	movie	6666
please	jack	oliver	success	albert

Chapter 10

Another Ten Password Pointers Plus a Bonus Pointer

Solutions in this chapter:

- **Password Complexity through Mangling**

Password Complexity through Mangling

Throughout this book, I have written about the importance of creating unique and unpredictable passwords. But I also advocate using passwords based on English words that are easier to remember. The problem is that English words are not unique and they are predictable. Even if you put a bunch of them together as a pass phrase, they are still quite predictable.

The solution is *mangling*, which is changing, distorting, mutating, or deforming a common phrase into something completely unique. Passwords that use diverse characters are strong and long passwords are strong, but diverse, long, mangled passwords are the strongest.

There is not much to password mangling. You come up with a password then go over it once using one of the below tips to modify the words enough so that they cannot be guessed. The ultimate goal is a password so unique that there would be a one-in-a-billion chance of anyone else having the very same password. The following are ten tips and an extremely valuable bonus tip that will get you started mangling.

Diverse Dialects

So, you have a strong common pass phrase but you are afraid it might not be strong enough. Would it be common if Elmer Fudd spoke it? Writing your phrase in a different dialect or accent is a great technique because the potential humor is easy to remember and the modifications are easy to remember how to accurately reproduce. Here are some examples of how you could use dialects to modify the phrase "I have fallen and I can't get up!"

- **Elmer Fudd** I have fawwen and I can't get up!
- **Redneck** Ahve fallen an' ah can't gittup!
- **Hacker** i've f4llen snd teh suck getting up
- **Toddler** Fallen mommy, get me1
- **Pirate** Ayyy blew me down matey an I can't be getting up!

Scrambling

Scrambling is a very simple technique; all you do is mix things up a bit. Move words around, reverse the meaning, whatever it takes. However, be careful not to mix it up so much that it takes you forever to remember how to type it. Here are some simple examples of scrambling:

- River—the Hudson

- To be to be or not!

- I'd rather not be not fishing…

- Please do not pool in my pee!

Slicing and Dicing

Pass phrases allow for more modifications to make your password truly unique. One technique, called "Slicing and Dicing," is like choosing a pass phrase and then taking a knife to it:

- near ly noon in norway

- im port ant in for ma tion

- betterthansli   cedbread

- thenut typrof essor

It is so simple but it works so well. Add a few spaces, take a few out, and your password is now unique.

Repetition

Repetition was mentioned as a memory technique, but it is also great for pass-phrase mangling. Repetition is so useful that I use it in some form in most of the passwords I set. It is easier to remember one thing and type it twice. Just make sure you are smart how you do it. Typing the same thing twice is a common technique and very predictable. Instead, vary how you repeat things:

- reallyreally long is reallyreally strong

- I'll…be…back…

- No way no how no one

The Replacements

Replacing certain characters with others is a great technique that is commonly used, but one that is normally executed poorly. It is not that clever to replace your a's with @ or your o's with zeros. As you build your password, think of how you would say it on a very long license plate.

Here are some examples of replacements you could do:

- Gr8 vacashuns

- go armx, go navx

- companee policee

- h&dsome frogs

Over-punctuating

Punctuation is the Swiss Army knife of pass-phrase mangling. Merely adding one punctuation symbol to all your passwords will do wonders for your password security. The whole purpose of password mangling is to ensure that someone cannot crack your password based on a common wordlist. There are many wordlists available, and some are quite effective.

All it takes to make sure your password does not appear on a wordlist is adding a few punctuation symbols. There are many things you can do with punctuation, including delimiting, bracketing, prefixing, suffixing, pattern building, and so forth. Here are some examples:

- After--->wards

- //lava//outlaw//

- Lenny-the-pirate.

- Mister :) AOL

- hide the ***** password

- --==//jetsons\\==--

- ......sleeping again...zzz

As you use punctuation in your passwords, do not forget about the special symbol characters mentioned in the Chapter 4. Also, remember that most modern operating systems consider the space to be a symbol character, so make good use of spaces as well.

Slurring, Mumbling, and Stuttering

If you have a speech impediment, why not take advantage of it to improve your passwords? Okay, you do not need a speech impediment to use this technique, but that is basically what it is. If it is unintelligible, it is likely hard to crack:

- th th th that's all fo fo folks
- ahmagonna gitta navacada
- Popolus rhodeisland
- The cccobalt mlion

Non-words

Passwords do not have to be "real" words to be easy to remember, they just need to look like real words. Fake English words are easy to remember, and you definitely will not find them on a wordlist, making them perfect for passwords.

- Kai's atmolingered wallet
- Sprained my forung
- 'Twas a complete outhacy
- Complete Pioforia

I never tire of this one technique. Here is a list of non-words to get you started:

Revitching, Sioter, Hassalic, Ephoich, Hasuxou, Stise, Ioxoaxay, Tisance, Eshasoaddify, Iaphouth, Hasoushi, Oumenoush, Ermenify, Dhapioz, Inxiag, Teencers, Oithoux, Tisechinph, Phoution, Tiarer, Ouhashane, Hacy, Hetisour, Wonnon, Forung, Emenis, Jhasoo, Outiofles, Thioquay, Souhas, Tiotheemen, Onrount, Tirea, Appleable, Tisominhas, Inzial, Shashafor, Menookings, Zoitislic, Qurettly, Hasoushedness, Thable, Inhasofer, Onzeaght, Etisizzy, Wuess, Eazify, Iahasosh, Achment.

Foreign and Slang

If you know a foreign language, throw some of those words in there, too. I'm not saying do your whole password in a different language, but mix multiple languages to increase the pool of possible words someone would have to test to crack your password. If you cannot think of any foreign words, try slang, especially something you would not normally use or that does not quite fit your personality.

- Bailando with Mr. Dirt
- ichi-ni-san-shi-five
- Grandma's warez dump
- Walking w/ the g dizzle

Typos

Typos in passwords are easy; it does not hurt to use them frequently. They are not a perfect solution because of the wordlists that are made up of commonly misspelled words, but they are a good start for mangling:

- Slay teh hyberbole!!
- Board 2 teers.
- blawing-mad
- Centralizing the sammon

The Long Anticipated Valuable Bonus Tip

Your password needs to be unique. It should be so different that you can be pretty sure that no one has ever used it and likely will never use it. How can you judge your password's uniqueness? You can't, but you can run a quick test to make sure you are not choosing a common password: Google for it.

If you search for your password and nothing comes up, chances are your password is sufficiently complex. It does not prove that your password is strong, but it does prove that it is not horribly weak. What is surprising is how many passwords you can find on Google. Many people find at least a few hits on their passwords, no matter how obscure they seem.

Table 10.1 lists the search results for several random passwords.

Table 10.1 Search Results for Random Passwords

Password	Google Hits
Brook55	2,290 results
20022002	25,600 results
baddog123	239 results
gizmo12	766 results
justin29	1,600 results
shark01	3,820 results
letmein	57,000 results
batman11	2,570 results
kahoona0	7 results
6969hune	2 results
salmongoat57	7 results

Remarkably, even passwords that seem somewhat complex still turn up results. I do not recommend looking up every password as part of your regular password selection process, because that has its own security risks. But it is helpful to try it on a few passwords to get an idea of what works and what does not. Go ahead; try it with some of your own passwords.

The fact is that people are predictable and hackers know that. Once you learn how to not be predictable, you are on the right track toward password security.

Chapter 11

The Three Rules for Strong Passwords

Solutions in this chapter:

Introduction

Everyone seems to have some advice on how to make strong passwords. Some of this advice is good; some of it is bad. I have grouped this advice into three basic rules: the rule of complexity, the rule of uniqueness, and the rule of secrecy. Use these rules as guidance in developing strong passwords.

The Rule of Complexity

Complexity makes a password strong. It ensures unpredictability and resistance to brute-force attacks. Complexity is a component of password length and diversity of content.

Three Elements

To ensure password complexity and augment length, your password should contain at least three elements. These elements have no specific definition, but they might include characters, numbers, symbols, words, or phrases. Each element is an opportunity for randomness. These elements can be loosely related and can sometimes employ repetition if used wisely. Here are some examples:

- Orchard/making-pies
- flour&eggs&milk
- 2crazy@doghouse.com
- Turn left,right,right

A Thousand Trillion

To protect against brute-force attacks, your password should allow for a keyspace of a thousand trillion passwords. Focus primarily on passwords that are 15 to 20 characters long with mostly lowercase letters to facilitate typing. However, also include the following elements whenever possible:

- Use uppercase letters in positions beyond the first character
- Use one or two numbers throughout the password, not just at the end and beginning
- Avoid passwords made up of more than 50 percent numbers

- Use punctuation and other symbols as delimiters or bracketing throughout the password
- Use spaces if the particular system allows
- Use high ASCII or Unicode characters when necessary for extra security

The Rule of Uniqueness

Uniqueness means that every password you use is exclusive to any particular system and distinct among all passwords. Here are some ways to make your passwords unique:

- Avoid using common passwords, common phrases, or dictionary words
- Never reuse the same password more than once, especially among different systems
- Avoid getting too attached to a single password
- Avoid words or numbers relating to yourself or your environment
- Avoid passwords that include personal dates or other significant numbers, pet names, relatives or loved ones, vehicle names, favorite sports teams, or other personal information
- Avoid using words connected to you that might lead to reuse
- Avoid using predictable patterns or sequences

Uniqueness also refers to uniqueness over time. To avoid stale passwords, refresh your passwords every three to six months. Never let any password remain unchanged for more than a year. Occasionally, change all your passwords at once, especially if you suspect a security incident.

The Rule of Secrecy

Always maintain the secrecy and confidentiality of your password to ensure its integrity as an authentication device. The following practices are necessary to maintain password secrecy:

- Do not share your password with others

- Avoid recording your passwords in an insecure manner

- Avoid saving passwords in Web browsers and other applications

- Always delete e-mails that contain a password

- Use a Web site's logout feature rather than just closing your browser

- Be smart with secret questions and answers

- Use one password while setting up and configuring a system and then change the password when the system is complete

- Always change passwords that are automatically assigned to you

Summary

To develop strong passwords, you need some guidelines to follow. This chapter covered three rules pertaining to the complexity, uniqueness, and secrecy of passwords. These rules will help you refine current password development (or creation) patterns and establish password policies that ensure your passwords remain an effective piece of your authentication mechanisms.

Chapter 12

Celebrate Password Day

Solutions in this chapter:

- Password Day
- Celebrating Password Day

Password Day

Password day is something that I celebrate maybe once or twice a year. It is such an important part of my password strategy that I thought it deserved its very own chapter.

Password day is an annual or semi-annual holiday where you still go to work, the banks and post office are open, and you don't get any presents, candy, or special recognition. What you do is spend a part of that day completely focusing on your passwords. Not just some of your passwords, all of your passwords—in an attempt to make them all unique. Go through every account, service, subscription, membership, system, and device you have a password on, and change those passwords. Spend some time improving your password selection skills, and securely document your entire selection of passwords.

The Origin of Password Day

I started celebrating password day a few years ago after working on an investigation that tracked down who had broken into a financial services company. The company had very poor network security—quite typical for that time—and had been the target of a number of hacker attacks. They hired a security firm to audit their systems and found that their biggest weakness was user passwords. Many user accounts had passwords that exactly matched their usernames, predictable passwords such as *password* and *administrator*, and some accounts even had blank passwords. They implemented a stronger password policy and slowly began the process of changing passwords and updating system security.

Six months later they still found themselves continually targeted by hackers, despite their many efforts to secure their network. This all culminated in a particularly serious attack involving the theft of sensitive customer information. The hired me to analyze their web server log files to track down the point of intrusion. After a long week of digging through gigabytes of logs, I found that the hackers weren't doing anything really fancy; they were logging in using the same means that their employees did—through FTP, FrontPage, e-mail, and VPN access. Worst of all, the hackers were using passwords they had stolen from the employees themselves.

Although the users now had much stronger passwords, they still had a password problem. The problem this time was that although they regularly changed their passwords, the hackers always had at least one password that still worked. They would use that password to regain access and obtain the remaining passwords. When that password would die, they used one of the others to once again regain access and obtain other passwords. Essentially, as they plugged up one hole, another leak would appear elsewhere.

My solution was to identify and change every single password they had, on every single system and device, *all on the same day*. For this company that was more than five hundred passwords. A week later, we repeated the entire process again. It was a lot of work, but that's all it took—the hackers were completely locked out and could no longer regain access.

A year later, I was hired by the same company to do some other consulting work and found that they implemented a policy to repeat this global password change at least once a year. Employees dubbed it *password day*. The strange thing was that they actually looked forward to password day. The boss bought lots of pizzas and everyone sat down thinking of cool passwords all day long. Not only did every employee change every password, but they were also given the time to change all their own personal passwords.

It was a simple security strategy that was amazingly effective. It involved users in the security process and was a good way to take care of those often-overlooked passwords that rarely get changed, such as router passwords or those for Hotmail accounts. No password, no matter how obscure, ever reached its first birthday.

Password day is very effective because hackers usually don't get all the way in to the core of your network on their first attempt. They gradually work their way in by gathering less significant passwords and other information and then spring-boarding their way to the more important stuff. Password day, however, effectively reduces the exposure to spring boarding.

Celebrating Password Day

Since that time, I decided to implement the same policy for myself. At least once a year I go through and change every one of my own passwords. It might seem paranoid or overkill, but there's no question that it increases my overall security.

The secret to celebrating password day is to think of it as a working holiday—a day where you can set aside all your normal projects and chores and dedicate a day or half a day to passwords alone. The trick is to make it fun; otherwise, it becomes a chore that never gets done. If you implement a password day at your company, make it a casual dress day, provide food or refreshments, gather people together into groups to change passwords together, or do whatever you think would make it more interesting. You might even want to schedule it on a day that is already typically lazy, such as the last work day before another holiday.

When you celebrate password day, be careful not to overlook any password you might have. Take the time to document all systems with passwords to save yourself the effort the next time around. In particular, watch out for easily overlooked passwords that you rarely use. The following are some passwords that might be easy to overlook:

- Instant messenger accounts
- Router and switch passwords
- Hard-coded passwords in scripts and other programs
- Service accounts
- Local machine administrator accounts
- Active Directory recovery mode passwords
- Logins for domain name registration services (such as networksolutions.com or register.com)
- Logins for SSL certificate authorities
- Logins for ISP and other provider accounts
- BIOS passwords
- Database and other encryption keys
- PGP pass phrases

Keeping track of all these new passwords will be difficult, so take advantage of password storage utilities like those mentioned in Chapter 7. When you're all finished, remember to change the master password for your password program, too.

Summary

That's all there is to it. At least once a year make sure you change every password you own. It will greatly increase your overall security and is a good way to lock out hackers who might already have collected some account passwords. Make it fun and make it thorough.

For now, password day is a quiet holiday that I and a few of my clients celebrate. Perhaps the concept will some day catch on and we will see password day celebrations all across the world at all organizations, big and small.

Chapter 13

The Three Elements of Authentication

Solutions in this chapter:

- **Multifactor Authentication**

Multifactor Authentication

Many years ago I had the opportunity to work as the security guard for a major film production in the area where I lived. A friend got me the job, and on the first day, he gave me my instructions. The film production company was renting a local resident's ranch, and part of the contract required that they provide a security guard at the front entrance. That was me. My friend dropped me off at the front entrance and told me he'd be back around lunchtime.

I stopped him and asked how I was supposed to know who should be there and who shouldn't. He explained that there is simply no way to know that, so I should just wave at everyone who passes by. He paused for a minute, as if he had never really considered this question, and then told me that if someone looks suspicious enough, I could probably call him on his cell phone.

So I sat there for eight hours, waving at everyone who entered the gate. Everyone returned my wave, and everyone seemed to belong there, so there were no security incidents as far as the production company was concerned.

Looking back, I sometimes wonder how many businesses have equivalent security systems in place in their own computing environments. If you look like you belong there, you probably do, right?

My wife has a credit card with her picture on it on the face of the card. When she shops with that card, the merchant can look at her picture to make sure she is the true owner of the card. Of course, her face alone is not enough to validate the charge. She obviously must have the card in her possession and present it to the merchant. She must also sign the receipt or provide a PIN. Sometimes the merchants ask for additional photo identification, and sometimes they ask for a billing zip code. Sometimes the cashier will ask for the card and enter the three-digit card verification system (CVS) code into the cash register.

If there was ever any dispute of a charge, merchants who use all these measures have plenty of evidence to back up a transaction. On the other hand, a credit card for a gas station does not require such stringent checks. In fact, all you really need is to have the card in your possession. There is no evidence that it is actually you using the card. They completely rely on the fact that you would report a stolen or missing card as soon as possible.

Any time you authenticate yourself to a system, you use one or more methods or factors of authentication. The more you use, the more secure and more reliable the authentication.

For years we have seen movies where the character uses a thumbprint or retinal scan as authentication. This technology, although still nascent, is widely in use today. These forms of authentication, called biometrics, can greatly enhance the reliability and integrity of passwords.

The Three Basics

Any form of authentication is based on validating one of these three elements:

- Something you know
- Something you have
- Something you are

Something You Know

Something you know is a secret, such as a password, that you can produce at any time for the authenticating system.

A password is an essential element for any security system and cannot be neglected. Although movies and marketing campaigns would have you think otherwise, none of the other authentication methods reliably replace a password.

The other two methods of authentication are very effective when used in combination with a password, but these other methods are not reliable enough to work on their own. The whole concept of multifactor authentication is to provide multiple layers of security that work together. For example, you should swipe a card and then enter a password; swiping a card in itself is never adequate.

As I discuss in this book, passwords do have weaknesses. They completely depend on the prudence and common sense of the password holder. Someone could steal and use your password without your knowledge, and knowledge of your password alone is never absolute proof of your identity.

Something You Have

Something you have is any physical device that can be in only one place at a time. This could include any of the following:

- **Magnetic stripe card** A plastic card, such as a credit card, with a black magnetic strip on the back that contains basic account information. The card might also include a code, such as a CVS code that is printed on the card. If someone steals the card, that person has the code, but this code helps prevent some types of fraud, such as stealing a credit card number from a carbon credit card slip. These codes also help verify possession of the card for phone or Internet orders.

- **Smart card** A smart card is a more intelligent version of a magnetic strip card. Smart cards have built-in microprocessors and memory storage, are generally more reliable, and provide somewhat better authentication than magnetic cards.

- **USB key** A USB key is a small device that plugs in to a Universal Serial Bus (USB) port of a computer. It provides additional authentication and often has large amounts of storage space for keeping private documents. A USB key might be a specialized authentication device or could simply be a USB disk appropriated for that purpose.

- **Dongle** A dongle is a small device that plugs in to printer, serial, keyboard, or other device ports on a computer. Dongles contain authentication information and sometimes contain encrypted copy protection routines. Software companies often use dongles to limit unauthorized copying of expensive software applications.

Something You Are

Something you are is the measurement of some physical or behavioral feature about yourself that normally will never change. Biometrics most often refers to fingerprint or retina (or iris) scanning, but much research has been done to use other methods for identifying an individual (see Figure 13.1). These include typing behavior, voice, recognition, facial feature, measurements of hands or other body parts, DNA sampling, or brain wave fingerprinting. And the list continues to grow.

Figure 13.1 Examples of Biometrics Include Retina and Fingerprint Scans

As I mentioned earlier, biometrics must always be accompanied by a password. The risk is that if your private biometric data is somehow compromised, you can't just go out and change your fingerprint every six months. Biometrics should be used only to enhance other forms of authentication.

Another problem with biometrics is that they are not perfect. They are basically a judgment call because sometimes our voices are hoarse, our eyes are bloodshot, or our fingers are injured or swollen. Biometric systems have been shown to exhibit some weaknesses and false positives. For example, facial recognition systems have been bypassed simply by holding up a picture of the target's face in front of the camera.

Multiple Layers

Using any one of these three methods is fallible, but combining two or more of them can have a huge impact on security. In fact, the U.S. banking regulators are requiring all U.S. banks to provide multifactor authentication for high-risk transactions by year-end 2006. Other industries are sure to follow.

However, problems are delaying the widespread deployment of multifactor authentication. The industry is still in its infancy, and the lack of standards makes some people hesitant to commit to a single technology. There are also expenses involved because multifactor authentication often requires specialized hardware and widespread software deployment.

It is an important aspect of security, but one that still has some growing up to do before it is widely integrated into our lives. In the meantime, keep your passwords strong—very strong.

Summary

In this chapter, we discussed the three different elements that we utilize for authentication, something you know, something you have, and something you are. Although this book is focused on building strong passwords (something you know), I cannot stress enough, the security benefit of combining this element of security with at least one of the other two elements, thus utilizing multifactor authentication.

Appendix A

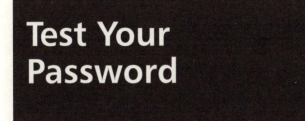

Test Your Password

Want to see how I would rate your password? Here's a simple test:

1. Is your password more than 15 characters long?

2. Does your password have a good mix of mostly letters and a few numbers and punctuation symbols?

3. Does your password contain at least three pieces of random information?

4. Is your password completely absent of personal information?

5. If you typed your password in Google, would you get no results?

6. Are you the only person who knows this password?

7. Do you remember your password without having to look it up?

8. If you have your password recorded somewhere, is it in a secure location?

9. Is your password less than six months old?

10. Is your password one that has never been used anywhere else?

11. Can you type your password quickly without making mistakes?

If you answer yes to more than nine of these questions, you got my approval! But don't get too attached to your password; once it becomes stale, you should trash it and start all over again.

Random Seed Words

On the following pages are random seed words you can use in building your passwords. Don't use these as actual passwords, but use them to stimulate your creativity.

This list is available as a download from www.syngress.com/solutions.

standard	space	provision	anyway
secretary	arrive	affect	visit
music	ensure	please	capital
prepare	demand	happy	either
factor	statement	behaviour	season
other	attention	concerned	argument
anyone	principle	point	listen
pattern	doctor	function	prime
manage	choice	identify	economy
piece	refer	resource	element
discuss	feature	defence	finish
prove	couple	garden	fight
front	following	floor	train
evening	thank	style	maintain
royal	machine	feeling	attempt
plant	income	science	design
pressure	training	relate	suddenly
response	present	doubt	brother
catch	region	horse	improve
street	effort	force	avoid
knowledge	player	answer	wonder
despite	everyone	compare	title
design	present	suffer	hotel
enjoy	award	announce	aspect
suppose	village	forward	increase
instead	control	character	express
basis	whatever	normal	summer
series	modern	myself	determine
success	close	obtain	generally
natural	current	quickly	daughter
wrong	legal	indicate	exist
round	energy	forget	share
thought	finally	station	nearly
argue	degree	glass	smile
final	means	previous	sorry
future	growth	husband	skill
introduce	treatment	recently	claim
analysis	sound	publish	treat
enter	above	serious	remove

concern	encourage	apart	speaker
labour	addition	present	second
specific	round	appeal	career
customer	popular	cause	laugh
outside	affair	terms	weight
state	technique	attack	sound
whole	respect	effective	document
total	reveal	mouth	solution
division	version	result	return
profit	maybe	future	medical
throw	ability	visit	recognise
procedure	operate	little	budget
assume	campaign	easily	river
image	heavy	attempt	existing
obviously	advice	enable	start
unless	discover	trouble	tomorrow
military	surface	payment	opinion
proposal	library	county	quarter
mention	pupil	holiday	option
client	record	realise	worth
sector	refuse	chair	define
direction	prevent	facility	stock
admit	advantage	complete	influence
though	teach	article	occasion
replace	memory	object	software
basic	culture	context	highly
instance	blood	survey	exchange
original	majority	notice	shake
reflect	answer	complete	study
aware	variety	direct	concept
measure	press	reference	radio
attitude	depend	extend	no-one
yourself	ready	agency	examine
disease	general	physical	green
exactly	access	except	finger
above	stone	check	equipment
intend	useful	species	north
beyond	extent	official	message
president	regard	chairman	afternoon

drink	partner	artist	district
fully	balance	agent	regular
strategy	sister	presence	reaction
extra	reader	along	impact
scene	below	strike	collect
slightly	trial	contact	debate
kitchen	damage	beginning	belief
speech	adopt	demand	shape
arise	newspaper	media	politics
network	meaning	relevant	reply
peace	light	employ	press
failure	essential	shoot	approach
employee	obvious	executive	western
ahead	nation	slowly	earth
scale	confirm	speed	public
attend	south	review	survive
hardly	length	order	estate
shoulder	branch	route	prison
otherwise	planning	telephone	settle
railway	trust	release	largely
directly	working	primary	observe
supply	studio	driver	limit
owner	positive	reform	straight
associate	spirit	annual	somebody
corner	college	nuclear	writer
match	accident	latter	weekend
sport	works	practical	clothes
status	league	emerge	active
beautiful	clear	distance	sight
offer	imagine	exercise	video
marriage	through	close	reality
civil	normally	island	regional
perform	strength	separate	vehicle
sentence	train	danger	worry
crime	target	credit	powerful
marry	travel	usual	possibly
truth	issue	candidate	cross
protect	complex	track	colleague
safety	supply	merely	charge

respond	painting	sheet	equal
employer	entirely	category	capacity
carefully	engine	equally	selection
comment	tonight	session	alone
grant	adult	cultural	football
ignore	prefer	museum	victory
phone	author	threaten	factory
insurance	actual	launch	rural
content	visitor	proper	twice
sample	forest	victim	whereas
transport	repeat	audience	deliver
objective	contrast	famous	nobody
alone	extremely	master	invite
flower	domestic	religious	intention
injury	commit	joint	retain
stick	threat	potential	aircraft
front	drink	broad	decade
mainly	relief	judge	cheap
battle	internal	formal	quiet
currently	strange	housing	bright
winter	excellent	concern	search
inside	fairly	freedom	limit
somewhere	technical	gentleman	spread
arrange	tradition	attract	flight
sleep	measure	appoint	account
progress	insist	chief	output
volume	farmer	total	address
enough	until	lovely	immediate
conflict	traffic	official	reduction
fresh	dinner	middle	interview
entry	consumer	unable	assess
smile	living	acquire	promote
promise	package	surely	everybody
senior	stuff	crisis	suitable
manner	award	propos	ought
touch	existence	impose	growing
sexual	coffee	market	reject
ordinary	standard	favour	while
cabinet	attack	before	dream

divide	whilst	metal	tooth
declare	contact	human	organise
handle	combine	widely	bridge
detailed	magazine	undertake	double
challenge	totally	brain	direct
notice	mental	expert	conclude
destroy	store	perfect	relative
mountain	thanks	disappear	soldier
limited	beside	ministry	climb
finance	critical	congress	breath
pension	touch	transfer	afford
influence	consist	reading	urban
afraid	below	scientist	nurse
murder	silence	closely	narrow
weapon	institute	solicitor	liberal
offence	dress	secure	priority
absence	dangerous	plate	revenue
error	familiar	emphasis	grant
criticism	asset	recall	approve
average	belong	shout	apparent
quick	partly	generate	faith
match	block	location	under
transfer	seriously	display	troop
spring	youth	journey	motion
birth	elsewhere	imply	leading
recognize	cover	violence	component
recommend	program	lunch	bloody
module	treaty	noise	variation
weather	unlikely	succeed	remind
bottle	properly	bottom	inform
address	guest	initial	neither
bedroom	screen	theme	outside
pleasure	household	pretty	chemical
realize	sequence	empty	careful
assembly	correct	display	guide
expensive	female	escape	criterion
select	phase	score	pocket
teaching	crowd	justice	entitle
desire	welcome	upper	surprise

fruit	beneath	these	while
passage	mechanism	people	point
vital	potential	because	house
united	defendant	between	different
device	chain	there	country
estimate	accompany	those	really
conduct	wonderful	after	provide
comment	enemy	thing	large
derive	panel	through	member
advance	deputy	still	always
advise	strike	child	follow
motor	married	become	without
satisfy	plenty	leave	within
winner	fashion	great	local
mistake	entire	where	where
incident	secondary	woman	during
focus	finding	system	bring
exercise	increased	might	begin
release	welfare	group	although
border	attach	number	example
prospect	typical	however	family
gather	meanwhile	another	rather
ancient	clean	again	social
brief	religion	world	write
elderly	count	course	state
persuade	hence	company	percent
overall	alright	shall	quite
index	first	under	start
circle	appeal	problem	right
creation	servant	against	every
drawing	which	never	month
anybody	would	service	night
matter	their	party	important
external	there	about	question
capable	could	something	business
recover	think	school	power
request	about	small	money
neighbour	other	place	change
theatre	should	before	interest

order	market	figure	around
often	appear	research	patient
young	continue	actually	activity
national	political	education	table
whether	later	speak	including
water	court	today	church
other	office	enough	reach
perhaps	produce	programme	likely
level	reason	minute	among
until	minister	moment	death
though	subject	centre	sense
policy	person	control	staff
include	involve	value	certain
believe	require	health	student
council	suggest	decide	around
already	towards	decision	language
possible	anything	develop	special
nothing	period	class	difficult
allow	consider	industry	morning
effect	change	receive	across
stand	society	several	product
study	process	return	early
since	mother	build	committee
result	offer	spend	ground
happen	voice	force	letter
friend	police	condition	create
right	probably	itself	evidence
least	expect	paper	clear
right	available	major	practice
almost	price	describe	support
carry	little	agree	event
authority	action	economic	building
early	issue	increase	range
himself	remember	learn	behind
public	position	general	report
together	little	century	black
report	matter	therefore	stage
after	community	father	meeting
before	remain	section	sometimes

accept	nature	amount	provided
further	structure	operation	channel
cause	necessary	human	damage
history	pound	simple	funny
parent	method	leader	severe
trade	central	share	search
watch	union	recent	vision
white	movement	picture	somewhat
situation	board	source	inside
whose	simply	security	trend
teacher	contain	serve	terrible
record	short	according	dress
manager	personal	contract	steal
relation	detail	occur	criminal
common	model	agreement	signal
strong	single	better	notion
whole	reduce	either	academic
field	establish	labour	lawyer
break	herself	various	outcome
yesterday	private	since	strongly
support	computer	close	surround
window	former	represent	explore
account	hospital	colour	corporate
explain	chapter	clearly	prisoner
usually	scheme	benefit	question
material	theory	animal	rapidly
cover	choose	heart	southern
apply	property	election	amongst
project	achieve	purpose	withdraw
raise	financial	liability	paint
indeed	officer	constant	judge
light	charge	expense	citizen
claim	director	writing	permanent
someone	drive	origin	separate
certainly	place	drive	ourselves
similar	approach	ticket	plastic
story	chance	editor	connect
quality	foreign	northern	plane
worker	along	switch	height

opening	massive	guilty	analyse
lesson	light	prior	anywhere
similarly	unique	round	average
shock	challenge	eastern	phrase
tenant	inflation	tension	long-term
middle	identity	enormous	lucky
somehow	unknown	score	restore
minor	badly	rarely	convince
negative	elect	prize	coast
knock	moreover	remaining	engineer
pursue	cancer	glance	heavily
inner	champion	dominate	extensive
crucial	exclude	trust	charity
occupy	review	naturally	oppose
column	licence	interpret	defend
female	breakfast	frame	alter
beauty	minority	extension	warning
perfectly	chief	spokesman	arrest
struggle	democracy	friendly	framework
house	brown	register	approval
database	taste	regime	bother
stretch	crown	fault	novel
stress	permit	dispute	accuse
passenger	buyer	grass	surprised
boundary	angry	quietly	currency
sharp	metre	decline	moral
formation	clause	dismiss	restrict
queen	wheel	delivery	possess
waste	break	complain	protein
virtually	benefit	shift	gently
expand	engage	beach	reckon
territory	alive	string	proceed
exception	complaint	depth	assist
thick	abandon	travel	stress
inquiry	blame	unusual	justify
topic	clean	pilot	behalf
resident	quote	yellow	setting
parish	yours	republic	command
supporter	quantity	shadow	stair

chest	initially	habit	sugar
secret	arrival	round	frequency
efficient	protest	purchase	feature
suspect	silent	outside	furniture
tough	judgment	gradually	wooden
firmly	muscle	expansion	input
willing	opposite	angle	jacket
healthy	pollution	sensitive	actor
focus	wealth	ratio	producer
construct	kingdom	amount	hearing
saving	bread	sleep	equation
trade	camera	finance	hello
export	prince	preserve	alliance
daily	illness	wedding	smoke
abroad	submit	bishop	awareness
mostly	ideal	dependent	throat
sudden	relax	landscape	discovery
implement	penalty	mirror	festival
print	purchase	symptom	dance
calculate	tired	promotion	promise
guess	specify	global	principal
autumn	short	aside	brilliant
voluntary	monitor	tendency	proposed
valuable	statutory	reply	coach
recovery	federal	estimate	absolute
premise	captain	governor	drama
resolve	deeply	expected	recording
regularly	creature	invest	precisely
solve	locate	cycle	celebrate
plaintiff	being	alright	substance
critic	struggle	gallery	swing
communist	lifespan	emotional	rapid
layer	valley	regard	rough
recession	guard	cigarette	investor
slight	emergency	dance	compete
dramatic	dollar	predict	sweet
golden	convert	adequate	decline
temporary	marketing	variable	dealer
shortly	please	retire	solid

cloud	judgement	proud	carpet
across	exciting	tower	ownership
level	stream	deposit	fewer
enquiry	guarantee	adviser	workshop
fight	disaster	advanced	symbol
abuse	darkness	landlord	slide
guitar	organize	whenever	cross
cottage	tourist	delay	anxious
pause	policeman	green	behave
scope	castle	holder	nervous
emotion	figure	secret	guide
mixture	anger	edition	pleased
shirt	briefly	empire	remark
allowance	clock	negotiate	province
breach	expose	relative	steel
infection	custom	fellow	practise
resist	maximum	helpful	alcohol
qualify	earning	sweep	guidance
paragraph	priest	defeat	climate
consent	resign	unlike	enhance
written	store	primarily	waste
literary	comprise	tight	smooth
entrance	chamber	cricket	dominant
breathe	involved	whisper	conscious
cheek	confident	anxiety	formula
platform	circuit	print	electric
watch	radical	routine	sheep
borrow	detect	witness	medicine
birthday	stupid	gentle	strategic
knife	grand	curtain	disabled
extreme	numerous	mission	smell
peasant	classical	supplier	operator
armed	distinct	basically	mount
supreme	honour	assure	advance
overcome	FALSE	poverty	remote
greatly	square	prayer	favour
visual	differ	deserve	neither
genuine	truly	shift	worth
personnel	survival	split	barrier

worried	fixed	corridor	dream
pitch	count	behind	alongside
phone	precise	profile	ceiling
shape	range	bathroom	highlight
clinical	conduct	comfort	stick
apple	capture	shell	favourite
catalogue	cheque	reward	universe
publisher	economics	vegetable	request
opponent	sustain	junior	label
burden	secondly	mystery	confine
tackle	silly	violent	scream
historian	merchant	march	detective
stomach	lecture	found	adjust
outline	musical	dirty	designer
talent	leisure	straight	running
silver	check	pleasant	summit
democrat	cheese	surgery	weakness
fortune	fabric	transform	block
storage	lover	draft	so-called
reserve	childhood	unity	adapt
interval	supposed	airport	absorb
dimension	mouse	upset	encounter
honest	strain	pretend	defeat
awful	consult	plant	brick
confusion	minimum	known	blind
visible	monetary	admission	square
vessel	confuse	tissue	thereby
stand	smoke	pretty	protest
curve	movie	operating	assistant
accurate	cease	grateful	breast
mortgage	journal	classroom	concert
salary	shopping	turnover	squad
impress	palace	project	wonder
emphasise	exceed	sensible	cream
proof	isolated	shrug	tennis
interview	perceive	newly	pride
distant	poetry	tongue	expertise
lower	readily	refugee	govern
favourite	spite	delay	leather

observer	progress	forward	instal
margin	grade	multiple	suspend
reinforce	exploit	outer	notably
ideal	import	patient	wander
injure	potato	evolution	inspire
holding	repair	allocate	machinery
evident	passion	creative	undergo
universal	seize	judicial	nowhere
desperate	heaven	ideology	inspector
overseas	nerve	smell	balance
trouser	collapse	agenda	purchaser
register	printer	chicken	resort
album	button	transport	organ
guideline	coalition	illegal	deficit
disturb	ultimate	plain	convey
amendment	venture	opera	reserve
architect	timber	shelf	planet
objection	companion	strict	frequent
chart	horror	inside	intense
cattle	gesture	carriage	loose
doubt	remark	hurry	retail
react	clever	essay	grain
right	glance	treasury	particle
purely	broken	traveller	witness
fulfil	burst	chocolate	steady
commonly	charter	assault	rival
frighten	feminist	schedule	steam
grammar	discourse	format	crash
diary	carbon	murder	logic
flesh	taxation	seller	premium
summary	softly	lease	confront
infant	asleep	bitter	precede
storm	publicity	double	alarm
rugby	departure	stake	rational
virtue	welcome	flexible	incentive
specimen	reception	informal	bench
paint	cousin	stable	roughly
trace	sharply	sympathy	regarding
privilege	relieve	tunnel	ambition

since	closure	clerk	everyday
vendor	automatic	curious	strip
stranger	liable	identical	stability
spiritual	borough	applicant	insect
logical	suspicion	removal	brush
fibre	portrait	processor	devise
attribute	local	cotton	organic
sense	fragment	reverse	escape
black	evaluate	hesitate	interface
petrol	reliable	professor	historic
maker	weigh	admire	collapse
generous	medieval	namely	temple
modest	clinic	electoral	shade
bottom	shine	delight	craft
dividend	remedy	exposure	nursery
devote	fence	prompt	desirable
condemn	freeze	urgent	piano
integrate	eliminate	server	assurance
acute	interior	marginal	advertise
barely	voter	miner	arrest
directive	garage	guarantee	switch
providing	pregnant	ceremony	penny
modify	greet	monopoly	respect
swear	disorder	yield	gross
final	formally	discount	superb
valid	excuse	above	process
wherever	socialist	audit	innocent
mortality	cancel	uncle	colony
medium	excess	contrary	wound
funeral	exact	explosion	hardware
depending	oblige	tribunal	bible
classic	mutual	swallow	float
rubbish	laughter	typically	satellite
minimum	volunteer	cloth	marked
slope	trick	cable	cathedral
youngster	disposal	interrupt	motive
patch	murmur	crash	correct
ethnic	tonne	flame	gastric
wholly	spell	rabbit	comply

induce	drift	fraction	landing
mutter	assert	whereby	exchange
invasion	terrace	pensioner	debate
humour	uncertain	strictly	educate
upstairs	twist	await	initiate
emission	insight	coverage	virus
translate	undermine	wildlife	reporter
rhythm	tragedy	indicator	painful
battery	enforce	lightly	correctly
stimulus	criticise	hierarchy	complex
naked	march	evolve	rumour
white	leaflet	expert	imperial
toilet	fellow	creditor	remain
butter	object	essence	ocean
needle	adventure	compose	cliff
surprise	mixed	mentally	sociology
molecule	rebel	seminar	sadly
fiction	equity	label	missile
learning	literally	target	situate
statute	loyalty	continent	apartment
reluctant	airline	verse	provoke
overlook	shore	minute	maximum
junction	render	whisky	angel
necessity	emphasize	recruit	shame
nearby	commander	launch	spare
lorry	singer	cupboard	explicit
exclusive	squeeze	unfair	counter
graphics	full-time	shortage	uniform
stimulate	breed	prominent	clothing
warmth	successor	merger	hungry
therapy	triumph	command	subject
cinema	heading	subtle	objective
domain	laugh	capital	romantic
doctrine	still	lifetime	part-time
sheer	specially	unhappy	trace
bloody	forgive	elite	backing
widow	chase	refusal	sensation
ruling	trustee	finish	carrier
episode	photo	superior	interest

classic	darling	secure	spectrum
appendix	decent	descend	intensive
doorway	liberty	backwards	invent
density	forever	excuse	suicide
shower	skirt	genetic	panic
current	tactic	portfolio	giant
nasty	import	consensus	casual
duration	accent	thesis	sphere
desert	compound	frown	precious
receipt	bastard	builder	envisage
native	cater	heating	sword
chapel	scholar	outside	crazy
amazing	faint	instinct	changing
hopefully	ghost	teenager	primary
fleet	sculpture	lonely	concede
developer	diagnosis	residence	besides
oxygen	delegate	radiation	unite
recipe	dialogue	extract	severely
crystal	repair	autonomy	insert
schedule	fantasy	graduate	instruct
midnight	leave	musician	exhibit
formerly	export	glory	brave
value	forth	persist	tutor
physics	allege	rescue	debut
stroke	pavement	equip	continued
truck	brand	partial	incidence
envelope	constable	worry	delicate
canal	filter	daily	killer
unionist	reign	contract	regret
directory	execute	update	gender
receiver	merit	assign	entertain
isolation	diagram	spring	cling
chemistry	organism	single	vertical
defender	elegant	commons	fetch
stance	lesser	weekly	strip
realistic	improved	stretch	assistant
socialist	reach	pregnancy	plead
subsidy	entity	happily	breed
content	locally	interfere	abolish

princess	working	basket	adjacent
excessive	chronic	drain	creep
digital	splendid	horizon	round
steep	function	mention	grace
grave	rider	happiness	theft
boost	firstly	fighter	arrow
random	conceive	estimated	smart
outline	terminal	copper	sergeant
intervene	accuracy	legend	regulate
packet	ambulance	relevance	clash
safely	living	decorate	assemble
harsh	offender	incur	nowadays
spell	orchestra	parallel	giant
spread	brush	divorce	waiting
alleged	striker	opposed	sandwich
concrete	guard	trader	vanish
intensity	casualty	juice	commerce
crack	handsome	forum	pursuit
fancy	banking	research	post-war
resemble	painter	hostile	collar
waiting	steadily	nightmare	waste
scandal	auditor	medal	skill
fierce	hostility	diamond	exclusion
parameter	spending	speed	socialism
tropical	scarcely	peaceful	upwards
colour	pardon	horrible	instantly
contest	double	scatter	appointed
courage	criticize	monster	abstract
delighted	guilt	chaos	dynamic
sponsor	payable	nonsense	drawer
carer	execution	humanity	embrace
crack	elected	bureau	dismissal
trainer	suite	advocate	magic
remainder	solely	slave	endless
related	moral	handle	definite
inherit	collector	fishing	broadly
resume	flavour	yield	affection
conceal	couple	elbow	principal
disclose	faculty	sleeve	bloke

organiser	super	antibody	strand
communist	funding	wisdom	stuff
neutral	shared	unlike	seldom
breakdown	stitch	terrorist	coming
combined	ladder	fluid	actively
candle	keeper	ambitious	flash
venue	endorse	socially	regiment
supper	smash	petition	closed
analyst	shield	service	handful
vague	surgeon	flood	awkward
publicly	centre	taste	defect
marine	artistic	memorial	required
pause	classify	overall	flood
notable	explode	harbour	surplus
freely	orange	lighting	champagne
lively	comedy	empirical	liquid
script	ruler	shallow	welcome
geography	biscuit	decrease	rejection
reproduce	manual	reward	sentence
moving	overall	thrust	senior
terror	tighten	wrist	lacking
stable	adult	plain	colonial
founder	blanket	magnetic	primitive
signal	nearby	widen	whoever
utility	devil	hazard	commodity
shelter	adoption	dispose	planned
hitherto	workforce	dealing	coincide
poster	segment	absent	sanction
mature	portion	model	praise
cooking	deposit	reassure	dissolve
wealthy	matrix	initial	tempt
fucking	liver	naval	tightly
confess	fraud	monthly	encounter
miracle	signature	advisory	abortion
magic	verdict	fitness	custody
coloured	container	blank	composer
telephone	certainty	indirect	grasp
reduced	boring	economist	charm
tumour	electron	rally	waist

equality	desktop	swing	cruel
tribute	saint	subject	diversity
bearing	variable	slice	accused
auction	stamp	transmit	fucking
standing	slide	thigh	forecast
emperor	faction	dedicate	amend
mayor	enquire	mistake	ruling
rescue	brass	albeit	executive
commence	eager	sound	clarify
discharge	neglect	nurse	mining
profound	saying	cluster	minimal
takeover	ridge	discharge	strain
dolphin	yacht	propose	novel
effect	missing	obstacle	coastal
fortnight	extended	motorway	rising
elephant	delight	heritage	quota
spoil	valuation	breeding	minus
forwards	fossil	bucket	kilometre
breeze	diminish	campaign	fling
mineral	worship	migration	deprive
runner	taxpayer	originate	covenant
integrity	honour	ritual	trophy
rigid	depict	hunting	honestly
orange	pencil	crude	extract
draft	drown	protocol	eyebrow
hedge	mobility	prejudice	straw
formulate	immense	dioxide	forehead
position	goodness	chemical	lecturer
thief	price	inspect	noble
tomato	graph	worthy	timetable
exhaust	referee	summon	symbolic
evidently	onwards	parallel	farming
eagle	genuinely	outlet	librarian
specified	excite	booking	injection
resulting	dreadful	salad	bonus
blade	grief	charming	abuse
bowel	erect	polish	sexuality
peculiar	meantime	access	thumb
killing	barrel	tourism	survey

ankle	diverse	distress	garment
tribe	revive	spill	material
rightly	lounge	steward	monument
validity	dwelling	knight	realm
marble	parental	selective	toward
plunge	loyal	learner	reactor
maturity	outsider	semantic	furious
hidden	forbid	dignity	alike
contrast	inherent	senate	probe
tobacco	calendar	fiscal	feedback
clergy	basin	activate	suspect
trading	utterly	rival	solar
passive	rebuild	fortunate	carve
racial	pulse	jeans	qualified
sauce	suppress	select	membrane
fatal	predator	fitting	convict
banker	width	handicap	bacteria
make-up	stiff	crush	trading
interior	spine	towel	wound
eligible	betray	skilled	cabin
bunch	punish	defensive	trail
wicket	stall	villa	shaft
pronounce	lifestyle	frontier	treasure
ballet	compile	lordship	attribute
dancer	arouse	disagree	liquid
trail	headline	boyfriend	embassy
caution	divine	activist	exemption
donation	partially	viewer	array
added	sacred	harmony	terribly
elaborate	useless	textile	tablet
sufferer	tremble	merge	erosion
weaken	statue	invention	compel
renew	drunk	caravan	warehouse
gardener	tender	ending	promoter
restraint	molecular	stamp	motivate
dilemma	circulate	stroke	burning
embark	utterance	shock	vitamin
misery	linear	picture	lemon
radical	revision	praise	foreigner

powder	inland	dictate
ancestor	beast	regain
woodland	morality	probable
serum	competent	inclusion
overnight	uniform	booklet
doubtful	reminder	laser
doing	bargain	privately
coach	decisive	bronze
binding	bless	mobile
invisible	seemingly	metaphor
depart	spatial	narrow
brigade	bullet	synthesis
ozone	overseas	diameter
consume	cheer	silently
intact	illusion	fusion
glove	instant	trigger
emergence	swiftly	printing
coffin	medium	onion
clutch	alarm	dislike
underline	jewellery	embody
trainee	winning	sunshine
scrutiny	worldwide	toxic
neatly	guerrilla	thinking
follower	desire	polite
sterling	thread	apology
tariff	prescribe	exile
sunlight	calcium	miserable
penetrate	marker	outbreak
temper	chemist	forecast
skull	redundant	timing
openly	legacy	premier
grind	debtor	gravity
whale	mammal	joint
throne	testament	terrify
supervise	tragic	
sickness	silver	
package	spectacle	
intake	enzyme	
within	layout	

Appendix C

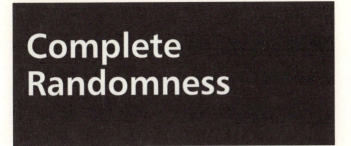

Complete Randomness

Because it is so difficult for us as humans to be completely random, here are several pages of random sequences to help you out when you need to be just a little less predictable.

This list is available as a download from www.syngress.com/solutions.

```
163  553  3i2  9y7  q47  447  890  669  S8x  4X8  29B  92Q  271  G48  667  791  171
355  949  c47  Q3B  924  844  824  988  987  616  791  Q37  584  j92  139  w48  842
4g7  7L9  YC3  6F1  237  944  8wc  332  156  286  w66  531  185  8WZ  gy3  288  815
148  aWj  856  972  723  k8d  298  561  P18  L17  476  5O8  841  869  712  I87  1S6
9t4  RqO  765  zRk  8y9  792  4o1  844  224  dT6  5T3  953  129  416  4SI  D3s  97u
332  2W5  s86  581  742  4C4  842  7w7  791  O87  t29  Z19  128  6hC  346  219  747
34L  gC8  J37  bx9  22b  536  139  251  sx9  161  56X  371  s35  254  8rD  922  782
949  Q2x  p96  65G  611  561  794  194  wa1  685  235  4v3  h2a  7t8  ty8  224  257
321  8B3  995  936  623  832  7p8  77C  811  345  341  696  328  423  936  j29  u6N
124  856  T27  113  B1m  IzD  3J2  d69  o2w  266  8g8  781  498  8c9  142  373  848
243  3AX  39j  ZO7  378  9r1  686  8U5  3P7  167  7R1  483  14x  725  872  159  93n
3n2  U12  69y  99b  371  639  475  1r5  Hv8  853  sA4  643  655  82I  6R8  L31  394
97p  5i1  45C  959  929  958  8d5  746  6Pr  7Hl  3on  863  MYA  95T  6tS  435  979
21u  778  1Vs  g3E  65g  11M  9x8  28s  9jD  48v  6N5  97W  6C9  335  ML3  93H  97j
811  8a8  67v  216  279  4h2  592  1k5  724  389  m47  4z1  412  o94  743  565  F1d
Oz4  1D8  8f4  y1k  2V2  2b8  x73  35D  3AZ  9w4  9j6  583  z7E  B35  953  947  329
5W6  218  616  m67  2aa  891  1c4  663  271  9v3  Vsg  8Tl  482  4cZ  513  MaV  L41
r4L  77f  p64  559  48f  37S  7x5  T75  841  2B2  625  113  g46  c48  13P  1W1  2on
5L3  x2B  895  64C  yV1  342  F42  h4v  1W2  76N  u9A  S66  sZr  76F  264  W73  953
4Lz  8UL  381  857  262  i3e  462  935  2B4  148  6S2  287  1w1  B74  v5Z  52d  2l1
7A1  218  27Y  7L1  6m8  517  816  6P5  VBy  2d9  187  qr9  811  547  547  4kX  985
819  923  87v  557  55q  G29  Z56  599  125  821  9EP  q63  83R  966  v77  8YQ  457
4fc  334  94U  21w  368  137  358  M59  71R  398  577  6X5  424  8Ii  7S6  7K8  3e3
42s  927  E75  Os5  16y  9Y2  156  451  z6E  474  34W  349  371  9O9  439  421  519
755  3dB  924  D84  154  y28  91b  528  o24  396  433  487  S19  oX5  179  831  B36
879  174  596  t66  T7M  79W  319  183  564  j56  1D2  n69  412  627  634  226  uN1
6e3  5By  196  555  19S  a41  629  7x5  4K9  993  797  L47  773  N3E  46r  663  91E
452  545  869  692  868  Iw5  898  8H4  f48  273  416  tR5  66q  J44  426  616  y38
952  7Q1  6gi  345  L12  382  7m6  p44  9h8  I5H  4v2  f47  118  l5H  p97  ta4  SEP
752  GR6  882  17B  614  477  1D3  Zl9  1oO  5c9  377  4JE  W37  2k1  4C9  484  7L1
Bx3  433  s92  112  812  858  639  q42  498  Y23  72z  3J4  967  27y  374  562  285
569  m2K  y3P  57C  R5O  413  625  793  83P  143  866  u93  o62  6H2  8P9  352  133
2q7  767  7YH  2Ua  2Uy  L49  872  47P  451  195  986  Z58  4j4  61p  e2u  z97  Ko7
x16  665  878  c93  446  424  586  f97  649  761  735  7p3  922  3T2  j24  P57  4K5
657  954  444  m66  b79  9aF  G73  422  22g  gU6  655  159  536  652  e86  189  9b6
ob8  959  1T3  244  7s2  o59  W47  276  Cl2  129  N74  66Z  246  2J1  1Xd  412  643
n8F  745  443  666  618  749  688  94b  5j7  2GN  331  K39  9mI  132  d76  a47  368
458  261  137  1D5  3w6  33y  J88  6s4  155  4z9  U11  L71  3P1  799  991  869  919
672  f21  hI1  3s2  A93  373  5p7  r99  245  118  393  A65  569  3x6  738  2O1  X1a
83f  267  444  428  263  84a  657  565  143  8X8  k85  489  994  18W  324  468  89M
P7d  341  p78  Z55  14f  t13  635  S29  34F  yb6  184  257  745  844  442  2N8  151
112  R79  294  m15  Vv2  61v  643  2R8  696  511  87C  43Z  6dT  965  T7k  424  E44
212  43z  33j  643  515  e69  225  77n  5O1  p34  412  V34  Nc9  K62  GX5  577  884
6J7  473  T72  232  7y8  m84  Cf6  638  k4v  55r  w29  871  221  D88  653  5i9  48F
575  267  126  nC3  h53  O3d  228  6kz  95B  677  236  944  852  388  377  U3I  877
143  AhS  3W1  277  52N  n14  764  4G8  64I  376  K95  262  L14  231  I56  Q65  H57
788  R89  C93  85q  H1A  3X9  U49  t42  155  796  4N7  23C  585  3T6  b77  72J  346
kX5  785  Dyp  118  945  75a  378  174  k29  m71  3e7  z52  12A  c38  676  cb8  f24
8b7  18L  219  119  2K7  6i5  25q  691  33V  7C5  FVA  366  96t  C45  172  G81  49y
```

```
336 A68 43Q 1M2 759 388 958 363 I51 z26 6Z6 Z93 C17 585 135 868 61z
40C 69r U6x 348 42i 425 821 319 3h6 623 54r 83j 16p 4Q1 338 782 998
145 315 AH3 448 769 7s7 6h4 891 575 71T 478 172 227 427 1wa 35T p13
232 482 2t3 7X9 2O2 22u 235 342 k55 298 qx6 784 98j 845 u95 5em 4G2
927 c4t 5X8 cai 594 26M Y3R 758 6F1 37C X99 2NV wE9 E4O 623 934 723
34k 391 585 572 559 l2n Fk2 N6T 1VW 7X5 y89 6m1 791 c28 U45 G94 159
59f 71C 411 33o g63 82v 2t5 552 126 emB 184 Z16 4yy 39H by7 VK6 448
cm1 846 n87 958 947 295 434 813 2L1 e52 949 756 447 w6D 428 775 265
f55 78C D4i 98o 282 L77 776 38h 842 354 QJ6 995 198 i41 EO3 485 271
N4s Z44 334 f39 589 pD4 f5v 7c3 467 Cz9 h21 168 398 797 Q33 4U9 59w
1To 314 884 237 631 5Gp 75D 238 58N 166 5V2 F88 k71 1LZ 774 Z2E 595
5AE 392 6lx r25 846 798 A74 L12 635 99R 56S M8i ZJ8 F4p 76O 7v2 665
95Q 444 8Gv 5X8 7I2 986 A92 262 14i o2S 687 771 832 843 o5K 45W W2P
452 T5z q65 4Zl 9S5 3Z5 497 565 4Z3 121 k47 854 933 6D6 KD9 94M R9a
1N2 4I6 773 6e4 946 473 77L XC9 m94 153 T8F 351 8X5 119 q29 A6j 4T4
5pY 18u u73 83q 177 u1F o25 867 24m 439 75q 755 493 383 915 223 88S
2HK 558 45l 951 886 93D 275 e87 644 236 222 4x1 13r U84 755 1W8 GgJ
212 448 216 t55 432 743 592 1f8 8j4 3j6 b8K 931 263 486 6J2 q99 J8q
474 bPO 4d4 4m5 2w7 615 768 1s2 N62 4I1 963 739 46C 378 257 2B1 x1w
234 645 3m9 P2q 177 765 Mk3 174 845 178 734 1r3 958 149 751 77W 221
8y8 875 Zk2 qQ2 xo8 5Y1 H1T 957 159 b9d 37O 4LY vk9 3b6 973 3Z3 K63
583 178 gm3 98Y uz6 11A 644 931 8z8 Z9W 724 d91 863 mMc 193 547 m22
851 769 31F 543 333 1d6 22V 6Z8 z5I Ij7 eH9 1k7 61s 9Z6 76X 969 192
rXm O51 637 878 w91 244 4X3 89F 557 829 932 754 131 57A 524 gC7 S11
468 8j2 t49 936 O19 8bV 577 954 1Vh 37O Vy8 5V6 387 29o 91X 612 3VJ
876 4R3 E89 Z8B 5p9 629 4z6 757 x36 295 Z6B 787 U6M LZ2 127 J99 7c1
J98 957 178 5IM 692 9C1 HZ9 186 94T 397 156 375 551 5f7 19O 9T4 855
381 PV4 334 1s4 O91 8c3 194 r8R 6jB 1HN F3P 585 b82 4J6 j99 764 226
56s 586 59F 48l a35 685 3X9 155 7Z3 Pe4 21T i76 1Q5 7o4 46G 1z6 J6x
5d2 C83 521 847 515 o99 185 867 ri3 647 68L f79 153 6D3 5Zw 646 178
3Z3 827 641 Z52 2xY 54k x41 Y94 671 4j6 t6i C2t 289 497 4d4 N9E 2wT
17w h18 586 jo8 356 652 482 1M3 18g S59 i51 8e1 363 F93 ig9 411 9J9
714 135 731 3Vb 544 736 9O4 873 834 156 84m 334 559 4D5 6I9 685 274
7D2 747 815 919 452 p26 N51 198 1B6 38v 485 865 94k 498 883 293 592
331 52o 896 363 112 115 764 8o2 7O1 345 9CQ 3g2 316 86F 6v6 54a 592
445 686 138 41D 192 368 9Fe f11 763 276 276 CD2 473 327 378 1EY 389
9j7 726 239 4NO 619 w43 975 75K 57B 339 721 S27 4Y7 211 e61 187 464
21I 519 68T 314 122 8I9 248 65P 34k 6r1 8s5 413 968 2j2 856 175 748
97T 391 836 476 V41 T95 b4E 844 849 z78 3A2 ej1 v49 418 228 G51 895
817 641 378 934 P47 394 Yu3 8K6 8Kj 528 44A 17d y2A 18j 647 y59 Ska
I9o 415 366 b5c 49M 511 648 87y 155 G39 754 722 848 8M9 472 6z1 589
KA6 38w 733 179 E83 651 434 571 69v 2f2 594 anx 113 748 313 35m 6Tw
4yi 8P5 327 5v8 5l7 9n1 175 28E 127 4d3 4B4 419 M18 W12 56v 161 679
8u3 939 e37 le4 515 194 122 s45 997 H12 s29 48O 3b6 K19 185 697 892
165 161 387 761 837 7dE 8Kj 996 47N 248 745 122 q61 659 281 55n v29
928 sIz 7g7 1T7 8W3 Gs6 16S 4s9 T2E 4i1 KQ3 892 75e 72N 5b3 757 875
816 A32 u4k 915 221 5H5 216 692 2A5 249 61O HU6 551 687 7m9 295 853
955 85h 873 783 635 931 851 715 461 861 QuH 231 585 74q 742 875 2m4
i98 433 4E1 874 596 3H7 116 337 963 434 459 4z7 D58 46V s54 JbF K75
```

```
922 m37 A61 727 882 615 563 5A2 778 13J 997 B95 6at 677 144 Q37 S6k
b36 C15 754 dL3 493 261 213 83I 275 3h6 257 86I Z87 915 W33 64f 1Z2
913 857 un1 15H 596 9B8 752 g8y 516 58d 394 555 677 757 Yp7 5gK 618
563 495 e3I i8D 214 d68 7x4 742 8U2 169 5P5 R37 ak1 c79 55y 282 t26
468 2A4 558 84V 11l 8f6 288 283 1g6 u22 247 38H BI8 l2y 136 jT5 185
2mD 911 h98 j74 o1a 14k 926 716 u24 vb6 5A3 928 42F 37m c28 3N5 13T
m12 4a9 U76 8m6 GH6 988 597 745 268 32F 656 4z5 3j4 345 H13 396 uB6
s1Q 56Z 1g5 LC3 814 426 9d4 456 2X8 NZ9 51d 52Y 812 311 4x5 459 Co3
em8 b49 159 F43 P67 1G4 D54 492 1v2 e65 6v5 wE9 31g 826 43j 364 338
9W4 7zY 366 7e8 8fv T82 Pl3 139 159 2hW L73 P9v O27 769 82R 5J7 825
9Y5 875 U27 e5q 983 6T7 4r9 876 342 829 134 15u 8I7 865 978 538 7Np
Y4c 895 L1f 332 13V lnS MW3 82j 435 X35 236 Zc1 6fx 896 854 5Q2 39v
455 73M 1y2 472 4rH 44v 423 2R8 y78 271 792 268 1z7 bac 349 6G3 l11
668 z1w 6Z6 887 15L 999 164 778 i18 292 539 836 431 c52 b42 u45 o37
l81 365 444 923 2H1 985 1r3 S31 7X5 143 693 738 733 668 2j8 Ga7 1N7
427 188 744 134 326 k19 173 8O9 17W m12 9z9 g72 71I Y98 6k8 72G 772
55u 925 Z93 H5N 7i1 142 288 617 4Ro 155 52j 597 83e 684 8k6 682 962
741 793 E43 415 98s 2U6 55g 99M 356 429 7x8 X33 854 B59 T7I 35E p3M
f94 29d 145 937 Wk5 6O1 93n 549 596 438 33q wq1 G29 127 8Kd 76f k96
8E4 71X m29 8A7 327 692 6H3 482 325 I85 Y13 743 715 Ud9 37V 518 4u2
38X 13Z 18g 842 98B 259 188 b75 255 w74 2s8 O95 31F i94 33u 364 c13
345 V88 I4H oh6 46C 825 623 581 U83 544 u12 882 57g 5ve 756 678 95x
6A9 16T 4I5 547 2c3 973 P83 T36 3D6 12V 915 k4y 9d2 267 27Z 915 56d
5k8 4i1 828 1v2 186 492 93s 579 36M 845 214 562 517 i23 Pf1 AKe 341
487 891 343 P25 s8u 457 88V 371 Sw8 2G7 56M 3vM 797 671 483 MI4 B8Y
487 914 496 87I 712 2r5 33b 5X9 9J1 9sm 566 74k x63 424 9Gz 115 741
6X5 56E UiA Flo 9J9 617 3W9 522 Fs9 935 Z2t 65F c48 61v 425 546 816
1L5 f26 987 8Cw 426 657 588 986 97z 967 KP3 512 56k e26 c96 v67 973
6k8 5M1 912 c2y 249 73B S86 523 116 73H 1v1 49F 641 D78 475 A32 6p6
V71 272 822 F81 z37 2T4 1m6 427 982 W42 478 m94 636 847 3z7 Y57 9s5
15q 6TE GE4 853 beZ TnL kSv 556 b22 62G 1a9 41L 63W p82 263 541 s51
587 P9s M1m h31 6L3 861 226 51d 587 31a 194 168 127 87F 274 2SF 38j
451 7p2 18z 748 937 3M2 7sw Sy1 731 P4k 6Ql YI6 257 626 e95 52h 676
42c 5g1 w99 943 b78 b79 883 674 85E 3Fr 752 ab3 377 327 2M8 177 6ql
22W 331 426 Y16 6N7 14n 35a W66 6R2 bW6 373 pk5 5s5 3aK 964 d99 879
371 231 398 36d 172 74N 34R 786 142 1Zf 68q g72 t3H 241 n45 562 144
739 4Ly 655 493 916 779 985 727 325 79f 6AU 676 27g 911 7J3 590 549
163 9k5 6H9 3Z2 i11 51E 463 72L 296 521 291 287 183 335 2h9 221 5p6
22o 6b9 D6I 213 298 g34 put 187 55Y 476 e44 293 R48 12J 3lx 176 779
638 32G 7G7 8v4 174 32X 225 698 18T C71 6Ld 155 2R3 893 78G 6e5 381
393 8uI 835 819 693 522 4y7 7N3 Z88 e42 716 479 59g 629 343 d66 L75
219 Cg7 35n 793 676 Kdf 694 2cT 961 75A 69r 518 352 8OG 855 149 637
182 122 267 M23 1J9 973 I77 872 v4X jR2 699 927 F74 527 643 327 5lz
Gj6 328 h4W P47 47w 235 539 Pm6 59B 99p 43S 874 833 L53 91d 375 6B9
d24 153 477 4X3 vE3 458 O92 OH1 5b1 764 64L 74N 3I4 618 6b7 28Q 824
179 Y2d 2G9 x72 64u 8S3 233 71z 3t9 818 434 599 355 o18 512 134 993
8wq 592 921 5A3 33X 567 Q6D C91 959 316 431 743 56W L93 75Z 661 8RV
147 I2n 52Z 4S8 861 113 594 o33 831 T79 i13 5h7 487 114 177 963 697
87Z Gu9 M78 kn2 s84 k2L 6m8 68q 8W7 486 658 3Lb 954 9J5 136 95f 131
```

```
3mk 841 826 8z3 67c 516 1ZN A19 Tr8 2T9 828 b86 7Q5 926 5BB cDB 7uF
438 381 699 45d 7E8 896 48D G64 2g5 945 g21 o95 71W 244 429 6i2 57K
28T 784 5i7 647 uZ8 31q DAz 34B 2p3 75i 693 J5q 471 UM5 257 1AV 3e9
i9R Ld3 443 U4Q 511 332 386 748 278 667 4U2 292 277 931 717 98K a77
647 44M D8i 987 3z2 VFh 11t 79J 646 5Q7 674 588 549 137 WZ3 226 d93
667 258 155 246 474 118 4F1 525 55u 522 871 789 6qu 787 26B wA8 8B4
6Z9 451 3n3 953 4a1 351 8J5 W29 9P3 F5H L86 zM1 929 152 697 S44 88U
283 368 h8G ZR8 7o9 B6p 921 986 f71 689 582 461 8Q5 t1l 358 414 291
418 9g4 1G5 69h 332 138 832 981 1z8 454 842 S18 8m3 9e1 M91 E55 M7n
125 524 852 6AW u48 M9M 976 823 284 76d 2P6 z96 FX6 947 13p 317 811
8D1 L25 357 7g2 219 8zG d2R 9R6 831 9W7 72z 6dZ bs4 181 754 388 654
X9R d14 626 564 7C4 45n 3z9 321 8b1 F18 E11 26G 889 Q27 555 544 5L5
857 h13 7Rn 638 17X i77 47P iE7 874 538 28N 893 5B3 s32 724 66N 164
961 Q44 672 735 8YB 887 441 jn7 r6n 199 717 589 4Z3 989 922 d19 687
932 43X Y75 s98 5TG 825 332 843 665 22a 851 896 345 357 585 b34 332
uIY C12 434 C14 4s3 3v3 273 8P4 qg7 689 59t 449 g5G g31 315 4O9 22t
gI5 84x 135 5f6 487 x35 568 g8m 1Ms 19N 515 6P1 bI9 685 692 1u4 889
388 25h N87 397 414 EQ4 j55 y89 1P5 d12 435 1s7 293 3V5 r55 27u 64s
94c 76P 125 154 h84 734 eu2 8ll 7N5 41k 951 413 865 199 w85 3x5 fz1
9rf 168 81m 888 521 77x 92f 9v4 495 8R8 h73 99s F85 949 1f3 47B 913
4R2 78e 9Cc J28 557 538 C87 356 17g 449 473 8F8 P71 K13 Ac2 595 317
889 F2G 226 r47 822 P19 891 375 e78 391 C8E 22C FHD 735 454 B24 119
7fI Z31 91n 714 925 r29 142 912 889 298 6x6 945 6v9 jY3 395 iW9 633
136 eV9 253 651 492 979 69y 475 642 AA8 1qW 985 491 S49 433 158 8Oo
399 489 6B3 184 7lr 839 286 e68 696 655 8W3 9S2 435 YDT r4K 62T 26W
953 92v 551 X9s 264 89b 127 MT1 H52 KFm 89I Yk9 C4y G99 577 Q59 4R2
882 F66 OHX 616 q5N 586 5c1 754 466 7BD 448 h93 71R 439 777 343 987
281 682 763 5N2 S56 n98 2sK o2D T17 C27 272 59W 723 E4Z 737 782 8Q5
831 918 1Y2 87D 276 255 8GN SS8 818 36q g11 596 9e6 437 374 e6V nij
612 652 416 7V2 c56 259 515 652 655 55c 6B1 921 495 pX4 17U 252 5c5
55m 812 858 zeX 61p 8i9 813 222 976 793 523 5q5 19M Hk7 2r8 928 n38
q79 26I 466 442 9I6 I27 392 49A 1a8 294 1dq 872 9U8 535 588 1k2 R22
8o8 463 7o5 391 779 436 885 448 W65 r9M 87j 273 v44 723 312 8M4 462
221 I9n 796 745 641 858 626 472 f44 4n8 235 3p2 6Q5 283 266 839 o8z
86u 61x 4w3 onS 592 658 349 9A8 6I8 c68 918 847 73X 64U 1R8 Xiy 775
878 89z v45 w64 6H4 727 848 297 484 7N4 289 44q 734 818 71C 291 25z
G62 572 512 548 5E8 7m4 332 y86 O13 7P3 372 539 2r3 872 8br C1A 115
y29 843 o87 H48 678 1T6 J3a 672 631 5f6 s92 E82 819 Q89 534 573 418
649 844 84E ohu 742 P92 885 71l 9t2 984 327 817 954 66D 221 149 44y
j63 177 9n1 827 15a o51 8f7 T54 4fD 735 3OV 49d Z57 494 oS7 33D 273
992 v65 6c9 C27 926 X18 85D 267 C11 523 55d 743 114 79z Rd7 599 457
94n 37J 84S L4W 42g 981 5g9 188 M97 74D 9H4 336 32A 477 388 I39 k3J
9w8 n25 462 518 758 ZBt 96M 541 928 d63 652 581 824 71L X44 eF9 2P5
865 R8v 223 426 229 717 J45 81A 55u 3a6 5X7 473 178 u6x 4F8 q3W 4W1
526 217 e87 48q 946 682 298 282 Qv1 6a8 271 5Y5 647 T45 32U 385 683
541 61s 94e 361 818 6q1 583 U26 45B 725 89W 4l4 8W2 224 412 934 396
T7I 5r8 421 313 138 16l 444 Z43 147 O71 377 7L7 6z3 913 G32 398 Yb1
613 339 639 h89 25Y 268 R42 987 575 1m2 262 133 212 264 691 P12 963
277 8Vp 365 o59 557 6Un 7yu 5y4 E55 2d1 6pW A34 864 176 243 FJ5 D32
```

www.syngress.com

```
757 D12 U78 N3K 8f1 O72 795 726 522 517 fy9 7R8 7KF 199 256 8X9 943
514 4Sw Q48 T39 35x 165 l71 PX5 5Ne 4Dl 747 562 771 2ce 176 kq3 EIU
452 2Tm 793 314 75V 953 277 D1X g4a J6b 91b a35 7o9 7D6 461 MH3 93S
328 6T3 751 L3M 988 757 194 455 823 wl5 348 516 519 7a3 48N 7p1 1Gz
244 417 nd1 vNs 3MK 3XI B72 C28 9h1 393 R49 899 813 219 2q8 319 933
b66 3AU p66 44L 736 67v x81 527 55K E28 3u7 h64 81s 428 7TR 24J 87F
191 K41 498 756 566 I71 757 344 877 158 646 Z76 Y4u 5YW 672 X2K 133
4tB N98 386 r34 259 X86 S2x I1A 28d IBQ 435 837 819 1z7 9p1 aS2 q64
921 Yc3 71w 961 5L3 993 917 558 236 468 e29 48X 3x2 2Z1 g99 Am6 294
910 948 B53 R21 982 855 4D5 453 187 479 511 6L7 v48 669 f14 31A 95g
897 8Z8 465 525 88I 193 K63 825 161 779 225 639 132 9qP 899 AAz 745
mm7 w44 b75 92P e65 8Cn 493 415 54g 559 3S3 34R h79 576 d6S 16Q qD7
4Ec 5wR 1gB 587 hd9 5Z6 4E7 345 5D9 Gq7 4Xs 363 t38 96I 8f6 388 3S1
63x QG3 596 829 434 G9T Hs8 956 f9h 296 481 7a6 748 e61 116 412 336
674 R48 513 N84 678 6e8 Ia7 S93 68O k86 7hb h24 137 54s 3PW c74 85m
215 831 1vj 995 89k 12R A79 311 965 Ya7 683 684 337 7b8 t61 2t6 o11
V78 697 611 758 y31 645 K77 663 5w1 93B 7gd 381 511 Y27 D1r 8i6 124
7d6 979 129 1T9 bW6 767 5FW xj6 516 525 4b8 6o2 226 3r2 752 yVi 16j
z78 H72 381 379 675 9r3 7V4 11K r57 314 764 C24 7F2 347 79C gJU 6e1
31N 363 m2S 755 439 449 139 E58 15I 557 N32 X3F 223 764 186 647 7a4
55p 324 634 a26 77E J92 239 399 761 U92 493 858 442 U54 55o 578 d79
51g b8u 2g3 2A8 219 y2V 9WN 792 H27 nK2 193 rvp 53h 357 7xI qs1 k96
518 D3p 2n8 888 46K 868 Q9S 388 1v9 38T 1k2 225 6r5 D96 492 4s5 427
619 211 551 523 6Y1 7p1 SL5 8I7 38k 857 672 887 867 9t1 486 936 t29
I93 252 29h i5F 34P 7Bt XGm 6gb aJ1 438 244 68s 815 21z 715 857 TV5
373 73g 87N 333 3v4 364 445 142 A71 z91 Ao6 123 376 179 5Z6 581 394
6W3 58n 5s9 54r 29c 8B4 853 OBc 927 q18 661 iN7 v4v 491 j33 4Oj T34
i22 758 64d 5u7 P6W 3Cp 183 6f1 129 411 771 732 95X 918 z86 s84 818
739 K63 di9 3K5 56G 28W 2n1 3J3 144 T55 Svn Q22 6OQ 242 559 M89 631
853 452 3e1 5l9 6Z6 9f8 11e M89 K72 da8 m31 1O4 462 129 46u 4p4 54B
83s G16 U48 878 286 3QQ g78 785 61d 756 6Z1 827 71j 747 N95 zpY 6o1
953 y17 24e 133 HL1 3X3 432 971 126 9Y9 26z 774 575 o97 4Y5 S92 e72
RE6 R7U 92q X62 67V 82P 7I3 76s s62 R78 91t 3h9 667 617 8l1 3Jq 594
C73 224 1N8 738 4Q5 489 891 Ye4 28s 2n6 e19 771 932 256 5IX 55S 5p5
L32 497 364 78o 411 292 39c 524 377 268 r59 96t 135 668 367 N11 5u3
858 z44 716 1H9 4g5 354 x85 47G 949 359 59H M9R 345 4le 48T 51h 511
164 KU9 3fr 585 B3W 813 92F 31w 285 e41 6F3 913 823 644 6Y8 643 97t
567 2Vf 759 n17 124 249 685 69E 641 9N4 766 479 FKv 2K1 368 V48 U48
847 813 8P8 8g7 V72 111 9W9 164 484 231 995 9O5 BrG sj9 922 Kb7 795
622 9Sn u84 9g8 6C3 m31 633 386 97R M32 na9 O38 358 sN7 854 876 915
62Z 112 531 158 848 93N 88Q D1E 62e 73Q dU9 6h9 555 88j YiK x73 675
189 917 4eL 8a3 26b J81 G13 834 326 665 624 569 889 5r5 343 II8 b5p
1S1 887 1J2 4I3 747 3d3 C58 372 828 74b 156 885 875 781 596 8T9 jg9
415 B84 E52 538 1N5 eLI 6Z1 b36 e75 835 171 3bR O48 6Z7 hE6 857 2tk
829 o3r 9TC 79O 37M 234 75A 86z 294 IC6 5O8 452 z76 o5k 23m 742 617
674 424 661 688 497 927 g18 758 411 9Sb 474 S83 7IU 3z3 2T1 D41 i56
CxI c46 7B2 W78 a85 L4R 9V9 884 485 76Z 529 V15 x27 556 443 373 55m
28U 659 118 623 h9v 19S D65 595 O85 352 549 892 744 4y8 8B3 a32 273
Ad9 9m2 769 63T 417 b9L 924 5q4 278 45m 26I 455 7p2 R51 Kp2 664 2b6
```

```
738 8p5 246 314 513 131 K3d 432 p37 163 483 376 7h4 138 k3y 951 979
4Y2 253 f79 142 9H7 6R8 642 452 345 e5p 358 724 Y15 99W 7b8 p88 5H2
452 8mK 3U6 229 3JR 9Sa 6A9 87D 718 1d5 w48 88R 8HZ 33o 997 162 56G
25r 323 241 419 2fh N42 8D2 c96 773 869 2J4 199 575 5pK Z79 357 192
4V7 629 96h 178 263 266 338 X94 418 fq1 99N 9y4 378 V45 2B9 H46 C62
R52 c26 7T5 439 849 532 F74 WM1 5a7 99b 8a7 981 2S6 c26 97t 886 42U
887 G43 e75 447 179 977 1F1 96w s77 1GC 2mv 251 s41 O51 314 316 198
693 XU9 498 146 125 X37 7Ul 748 725 257 244 952 57o 3C9 285 56w 58i
R5k 52A L91 331 y65 95G 372 26s 8q9 f31 Fo6 851 k4a 249 698 2K4 124
744 477 2vI 844 7u9 562 157 1s5 699 4R1 619 899 437 227 761 813 959
235 Vx1 62E NT7 Pm4 7b8 94x 856 4y9 541 3q8 8o7 391 84Q 213 F63 11H
68H 46B 422 941 42s 158 64R 927 981 541 S17 463 169 489 97u 583 z15
54L 251 26C 815 6r1 5f7 621 9I3 269 w29 125 262 K76 735 z73 neR 369
937 e3w 1ns h51 Mq3 88r pq6 973 5a2 79g P5u f76 642 231 118 w93 8l2
148 g77 892 999 93j X49 152 658 53D a33 B24 123 R12 ci1 63g 819 kRK
32t 76N 958 947 863 8Gm 3a2 S28 hY2 216 1o5 746 954 bEs 188 167 8J4
767 818 G16 D14 mw1 27A CaB 39I vZ2 8U4 878 857 q98 SY7 E71 2Y1 178
921 93n 974 135 3O2 U23 745 8A7 83z 927 494 h4x M97 429 487 881 671
c55 855 674 851 9s2 8iY 64C 962 f81 k78 267 161 192 713 257 841 379
q8f 4V5 58q 199 c53 Z91 C65 6f6 697 a18 cuu 912 a5o rR9 579 dAO 481
mv5 Fn9 784 685 74K j51 k23 163 E91 384 6f4 V98 I9i 9gM EN6 66U 24G
818 978 194 644 311 385 856 2ll 771 7i1 V65 6R9 74c 8L4 2F7 F82 94z
423 ah3 418 8a4 4XT 87q 83g AqQ 1Dc 474 9J8 11q 243 738 812 454 496
119 I93 2a8 m82 248 1a3 754 958 678 n57 692 86y 987 783 457 2d2 Lq9
243 G1O 62C 978 814 343 778 3q6 597 u7d 1g9 324 315 3az 7W5 78D 51t
1iq J3s RR7 816 256 B29 59o E55 9YP R7x 764 1q7 8S1 6QU 367 662 311
672 338 Gz1 C4g W45 524 482 143 33u 9N3 F16 x24 341 127 78y w4c 4X4
967 4h5 4Cz 47J B82 68e z49 965 534 55T 532 6M5 489 276 N3v 91p 496
744 f36 hh8 434 428 j92 17U 791 766 9p5 SCO Q39 383 471 U16 341 29i
S8b 932 199 4Nj 761 576 587 92d 7t1 379 47p q53 S19 832 457 89L 518
322 450 rs5 452 W92 432 79n Q93 628 L78 7w2 537 f9K 322 254 a75 98W
818 784 Js9 695 6wD 26q 258 247 874 NW7 164 y37 19F JV4 185 B15 1R9
68x 3q9 825 5Q8 6H7 l15 56r 828 12Y 118 792 2P5 512 e91 U4v 314 3X7
2S9 153 N58 1o2 65P 2K7 799 35N qY3 3r6 38p 844 443 838 369 976 7g4
D23 863 48G cLC 3J7 861 S84 s91 922 bgF 7p3 Q11 175 554 471 769 793
17c 5sO Y21 86r 152 78I 665 25c 182 N5W 279 o6A 187 5c9 765 mm2 86I
69r 891 467 g36 C48 6j8 888 Ph2 317 864 2P1 292 812 i5v 7y9 7U7 181
5o7 996 C3Q 97j 2Wu 2r7 319 391 7Y5 X24 967 3P6 p43 738 7m4 7oz 396
SZ2 x77 18n 341 5z1 X66 4E4 14I g63 857 678 o48 181 695 lXu 493 542
175 B31 495 481 281 313 79A 78q 442 41f 666 939 f72 T8F 934 13w 588
we3 2i1 K83 13d 796 914 H33 323 316 wrs T74 b57 7O3 631 4k7 239 999
47e 736 993 391 1g5 w76 454 898 727 a74 22j 7c2 77J 252 38t 563 j57
5Q4 487 Rz4 c29 94d E88 956 941 495 68p 513 6w2 5Ou ZI4 639 D96 4c3
296 27v 2OH rd6 437 Tx4 71t 5c6 i16 975 z42 386 323 9VF h54 489 934
5o6 MS7 QT1 214 9Q7 758 616 28Q a49 63Z 848 588 58J 27g 333 811 C87
G98 u71 848 111 455 91T 659 361 973 691 585 1f7 561 352 98i 75q 355
a55 966 x4R 864 53h 118 a3J 8D8 466 8G7 335 ye9 583 1Q2 44r I6a Q94
774 582 Nb8 168 r37 f45 yj7 8n3 S6J 5R7 17b 982 947 DW3 8V5 E4d 461
o19 n96 817 c61 596 i99 872 73C c36 372 9GU 71X 4B5 J34 115 113 376
```

www.syngress.com

```
R82 Pc4 427 p68 1d8 434 842 647 69k i24 X38 347 24v 449 Cg5 8s2 221
q64 725 5o6 629 57I 284 2r8 25I 7r2 662 183 5Uy t34 141 2H2 W93 7Pl
949 65S 73n 186 68b 298 88B K5M r1N 66R 6JE 741 W63 182 984 857 22O
8H8 n11 124 226 539 652 54d 58z 853 7D1 5d3 995 v1y 992 v88 578 313
71K 337 941 D13 c86 C55 99N 459 45Q 228 u84 c65 247 F63 4V1 436 44D
R81 h19 658 146 pX3 729 251 987 9z3 4G2 2L1 634 49G 874 788 731 To1
715 376 864 uzn 172 553 985 422 95F 19u 662 R81 9AG 651 134 w15 u19
8W4 94s 776 413 98V 1u3 1bA 388 j3o 5Fc w51 G82 515 692 3d9 4z3 6fJ
23v s6Q D75 5sX 9ko 2g8 z32 4B7 z8g 382 7J5 783 9K9 b56 697 c38 mF2
9q6 215 772 O94 772 933 812 e15 2n2 461 2og 3m3 821 7h7 2X5 Z42 927
2c6 9r2 235 328 855 776 3Z6 J81 N13 228 x87 e61 643 966 823 234 6h4
831 4mS 514 428 855 8g6 654 223 K79 Cg5 275 2nL 3S7 755 89J 861 79J
839 61P 826 13z 7y4 63o t59 4b3 1e2 q9O 5S3 5Z9 156 85Y t46 m65 995
k81 536 vB9 p7a 31K 986 oSC 93t 873 577 1Ad 34c 719 862 665 F73 186
761 5n5 565 64b 4z2 i3u 84l 9a7 s84 x96 2K2 W46 899 649 2u7 975 62v
46s 192 p1T 662 Gh9 54C 721 535 211 764 71g 153 873 4w2 434 1k2 2j8
562 576 b82 7L8 91F s81 281 925 N44 629 835 6yr H19 892 X63 416 7qC
483 3F2 7A3 c7Z 13G 839 641 63p S14 984 e79 254 e57 461 1x6 p19 65O
6C7 153 U92 A5H 973 9s1 D38 3A5 745 676 g26 729 T13 438 7f6 861 F94
62Z nq7 938 134 217 611 r23 63y F98 285 895 v11 B64 975 499 O15 84r
3rC 5xn 8L1 h1S 487 356 956 862 4O6 L36 E68 768 B75 NH8 671 595 8G8
M67 628 283 9a7 6B4 1s5 k9z 238 4y9 3G3 973 527 771 261 666 848 N11
64m 41U 78K 6h8 m13 4Cm w6R d42 j95 437 7g3 498 oI1 888 54F 2n1 Y43
37N 5qK 77U x57 492 x41 188 6R4 8s6 5e1 kc1 W94 623 5W7 966 923 92U
764 a41 2YF 4zC 2D9 572 557 4z8 6r6 C26 182 837 Cbh 828 951 SP6 n33
712 9g4 dv3 Z41 343 7k2 145 151 965 Uy1 157 S8S O66 374 56K i6t b59
z35 4hq 737 roT JsF 263 924 325 1D8 W29 186 2XR 2F4 559 44E 9L8 71j
11x 288 n48 736 226 851 898 z3q 14D 1zR 756 792 182 8Gx 311 591 vZI
519 397 8D2 68G 566 4z5 554 3HY 94u 356 484 36C 133 y85 146 22k 23w
924 392 51o 1fl 278 911 176 619 258 3I5 926 693 954 783 4e8 1L3 3q6
7D3 o5l 261 4n6 78O 674 517 51l 98r 6N7 472 9g2 363 7A1 9dZ G28 25F
1S8 219 1F9 131 KjS 129 kx5 582 7m3 223 66U 18F Qc1 342 195 8j1 143
356 7CT 562 793 527 6R3 1b1 631 f71 j9a 66d 753 523 1V7 444 XP8 939
766 6F8 488 512 62M 423 228 248 v7l 343 rC7 58t 422 x3F 7p2 7XY 241
593 6d6 D27 ZE8 15t 691 x49 M48 645 997 819 r32 A76 4u1 188 qTA C47
549 9W1 O44 495 p47 74R PL8 3i8 356 9um 1K2 348 2y9 437 6r6 79B 441
766 23H 7J1 155 q93 253 778 O6D 155 5I3 52C 3fb F35 J68 867 84K 37O
p34 PT1 782 74F 929 7T8 465 273 t3d H31 43r 311 81B 3v2 574 23T 1i4
899 956 586 664 KN4 6k5 296 172 397 614 12S 518 9R4 753 7w3 999 795
339 2X7 477 Q5g 195 486 258 223 1CP k35 4H2 417 594 774 574 989 756
3Dd 178 97U P3U 355 664 973 351 9J1 325 4K6 846 839 48I p94 851 K29
U7Y 885 876 968 913 I12 184 924 w8Z 42S 861 21R M7s 692 255 NUr 66q
oH6 qc5 ZI9 6E5 8j5 9Y6 242 377 4g7 F91 791 L8o 598 477 61e 953 T13
P97 124 4E5 J6o 887 623 R69 2K1 376 3yg h53 499 Q89 5vD V3t 96d J72
634 jW8 83c 457 1G4 9r8 91E O86 p2w 943 32f h82 R76 556 3U2 186 399
6Zr 714 2T9 b28 6d4 215 5n9 698 58O 245 38D 181 629 fk1 C7D w33 597
456 g6o 8u1 1uS 393 885 2J4 Kjg 252 971 sW3 697 51P zmi 523 589 c8F
786 261 L83 W7V h15 432 1W2 2m6 I49 867 116 917 c2I 51V K35 b8N 524
97p S66 V9M 9U1 935 37G 751 535 653 29c 5i8 p83 15c 31q 367 2G6 K2c
```

```
9q4 322 S77 128 K22 493 242 362 q83 76t 31r 629 3Rp 467 h76 945 29K
33X M9y 117 161 125 6J8 822 28g 599 698 9uc 8A4 127 27h y86 458 73f
8Gn 859 844 611 79y 326 2S5 k88 81b m2c 6S7 g38 ES5 6wd 485 487 97L
7z3 178 953 kI6 766 N77 i83 n44 46n jo1 Q73 2r4 y14 484 385 O94 44S
4Up H43 1U4 839 7A7 g8Q W3M L38 3v2 272 918 26v h54 b94 37L 843 5F1
227 36n h98 F81 368 9a6 353 d68 7Q3 191 y29 386 9D7 485 IU9 vm2 5Z4
pw3 S43 Q1j 842 7B6 34I 676 9X3 49M 35w 558 617 1Tx 553 835 h6c 941
u32 146 37i B62 824 941 527 581 337 H77 533 7p9 163 714 518 3A9 681
S7t 63N 838 u43 9nQ 892 55P 649 667 4H8 Yq7 s87 299 497 7F7 1y9 ex7
6Z2 6j9 5D3 N37 748 661 dA8 1s8 473 17r M5o 6N3 Dc4 9cn 5V1 146 648
714 u4t 319 889 674 863 43F C2T 3u3 342 428 2X1 168 q4i 183 12o 8h9
956 4e1 267 883 43H 394 4NQ 652 914 Pe7 292 6MU a85 1K8 54x 186 a46
5or 579 5E3 2L5 53n 565 285 796 787 192 6G9 2Xs 8Z3 214 471 243 2rs
382 9r9 12q 498 821 429 V69 S94 WD4 i92 772 9CX 941 20s 372 G48 518
965 433 F31 g45 588 8g8 213 746 913 372 559 782 622 192 8z1 674 r69
121 976 I54 924 Y44 855 a8O 636 923 2w3 646 j71 51n 129 662 59d 72j
7s7 xp2 125 81e 5I3 49d 362 737 3sk 8D5 1Y4 892 8E6 685 Y6Z 155 774
xv9 691 41l 179 1Q8 K7i 6IT 85h 365 W26 3a1 XL1 aH8 84D 268 1X6 2fd
672 142 31T 3e5 42d q93 57J 828 5w6 482 154 8Xm 83W 425 547 7Y3 695
688 g27 482 Y49 464 827 a41 L93 82K 2r5 911 259 363 3ro 9A8 m34 656
5X6 167 a2Y E93 976 P5n 173 j85 647 254 349 562 274 682 2K9 184 295
389 771 Q18 xe1 292 7v3 3z7 5NX X12 u19 AE7 539 K52 268 3Ny B59 F33
3T1 6v5 5m1 287 2q2 X7q K91 643 52p UJ3 K3m M81 885 14H k29 947 823
15z v24 X11 3GK 135 n93 U57 4T7 185 426 i92 55u 3L8 392 5VO Ui7 F85
127 5M6 385 11w 333 531 179 44I K8K iR9 q76 116 883 Y62 O31 888 47K
2Hr U14 9Y8 A51 25x 411 3dL 3kC 9k4 663 671 7ig 53Z 7O1 372 843 83e
595 27T 424 R34 4J5 849 566 F45 593 582 O71 1i2 852 276 C31 v73 JPj
649 R77 k5A 83k 519 679 911 847 366 346 T18 gR5 237 157 nu6 B48 413
826 q85 397 u79 4pY 8F7 291 1bk y73 9V7 92H 222 818 415 272 n8l a28
568 j94 6aC 2O3 6fp 77f 1Am e95 Ud6 p18 17e OA2 92G 841 529 m59 w95
8K8 69D 373 E6h x35 212 389 113 j2s 17L 544 J82 P26 O78 1Y3 972 189
O59 623 819 t6j 261 N51 O92 3V8 4L2 672 45m cQ4 468 N3G 463 787 523
819 475 775 M49 789 u9x 535 B12 755 32i 2Ty 125 621 4vT 57Q 355 233
5Q3 614 938 c66 634 8t6 87S 527 77J 9n2 817 X83 dz7 7o7 316 624 9P5
h96 34V 92m 4N7 j21 f33 416 2Q1 44e T97 165 J2N yRZ 644 H15 791 426
19A 53r 59d 38k 1QA 6H3 H59 A76 558 FA4 vj5 24V 775 21x P95 6k4 786
f98 667 19N 754 3JQ 868 4M6 824 694 642 mT4 46i j3M 45H 955 1V9 56W
922 81e 861 o55 5B4 212 87e k3u 782 179 692 r3v 58o 4Cu 1X1 I45 615
1P9 8E6 892 w76 255 r17 4G3 333 976 581 867 V7b 2R3 354 75h 226 23N
543 719 629 438 1A4 928 kr8 Pb7 3qG y2k 485 386 277 V47 837 bGe 241
2A5 333 e71 156 vG6 m86 6Ag 886 947 994 67K 193 39s h6U 54J 8J5 3u5
692 S63 5U8 vL3 8v8 d61 76S 529 N58 134 639 4SD t11 9H4 93K a73 589
2q2 279 514 914 379 677 4e1 298 429 464 229 V6j 875 o81 935 53C 1s7
UEP 347 ND2 p77 132 8z5 566 1D5 586 D48 r34 517 673 X64 Ju8 47r 3o6
447 391 8M1 8M8 383 345 749 J31 92Q r48 286 43A 864 12x 935 6eH 188
w58 869 O68 257 9K8 293 t29 882 871 12b 375 M39 3a4 k96 726 Yi3 u32
132 V88 492 215 1z1 912 81b 724 336 qd1 363 98o h88 Kpr 493 U5z 447
793 411 s22 X72 292 7e1 755 298 70o Ar5 R35 592 8g4 9E3 T27 G66 5NI
s57 586 893 128 2V3 9D4 61Z 914 327 233 43o 368 3c4 5i6 DPs 257 926
```

```
9E9  w15  8T8  Kg5  U76  cT9  72M  Ak7  51V  945  t99  4R8  k4H  819  74c  1wM  hH1
995  z79  A6z  5oF  165  55Y  887  19L  G46  8x7  86d  EW7  G56  7hw  4GQ  87G  T92
439  69d  1rG  21z  86F  1AB  226  5X3  433  X9p  U44  Q77  r39  Az6  4UX  198  985
515  622  QT2  4a9  277  917  723  3n2  78U  3V6  354  777  714  9z1  f64  p98  a58
827  27Z  398  6x6  Q61  94S  18K  6ej  822  62J  779  833  nj7  p11  651  871  U69
599  Uq8  931  752  52y  4m8  569  578  88R  949  184  215  4r1  522  839  74L  319
9g8  2h7  1e7  i91  911  482  365  484  487  0tv  184  515  h35  535  3FY  8Wv  228
K55  66c  36p  976  947  6r6  216  6H4  42i  Q98  367  918  812  6q4  694  248  765
3i1  86A  297  B32  786  9L8  42d  486  w52  277  E93  G45  4H4  N77  829  39S  Jm4
5u1  632  1D2  n27  857  B57  39m  178  p73  757  Tn2  152  9Sv  355  88l  748  354
294  Y66  9n5  SR6  51l  724  B17  8C6  127  895  857  795  613  7b2  117  833  1vu
5V4  453  f39  377  996  3U2  84h  9l5  329  6ny  r4N  5ER  169  8C6  i71  29K  3u7
i55  e84  449  H47  811  439  Bt5  869  f45  155  Qh1  W83  735  355  3q9  652  972
b18  1s4  5ud  r76  3a5  g88  187  353  K81  935  1sf  989  752  596  r22  5o8  596
37T  729  518  871  261  9y4  869  27W  P1s  j6A  517  846  5ow  63a  535  223  65B
827  583  64u  636  H73  4ib  424  455  r25  9C8  Sa2  47A  492  638  339  al7  138
929  448  318  5k8  J37  852  54e  934  78a  2al  144  36L  l51  799  584  37z  797
66C  4s6  92C  794  mA7  1v9  567  9l5  285  je6  752  261  82W  9v3  89o  242  178
Dgw  89j  889  651  o86  5lo  l41  43Q  755  97e  5JC  976  FC3  75D  46B  221  881
2U1  623  Pk1  Tq1  i9d  295  u19  238  iOx  181  m8j  22N  2Y5  798  456  671  797
466  472  OO2  596  52W  185  8c3  t2h  3xj  952  7Z6  8C5  475  12P  839  456  f49
1x5  753  77R  tp8  k46  194  35q  258  175  699  193  23S  f97  9oM  98w  694  Qfh
47z  a68  54c  5r6  m62  W45  11y  7v3  W7D  515  N42  797  54U  8i2  Sx6  e41  454
5R8  332  9V9  982  41n  17G  941  625  558  7h7  6I2  169  V67  R71  P44  366  r82
c1n  395  323  525  5s2  48S  178  96O  436  764  656  q68  K57  8Cm  326  661  8p5
243  Q18  H67  368  e6L  3c4  h7K  N79  n23  5W5  539  7m4  852  gj8  521  373  746
54g  71L  c93  7W6  415  V76  15V  336  V74  3L6  Ah8  144  381  65P  Y77  K26  987
466  687  g9b  562  274  1K8  615  w86  484  889  454  x43  315  c1l  4Z7  159  327
b52  i32  5p2  743  b93  859  546  3X9  476  111  77D  7ea  53k  d2u  x38  88O  b11
6R3  j92  o88  1m5  645  986  833  15Q  13N  V77  23Q  62E  495  6r3  3I1  87p  784
9l2  6E4  524  G54  985  wg2  57Z  348  225  8E1  i25  O25  j46  329  3W2  59I  k46
8Q4  5f5  cIG  lJp  312  2Gv  386  bdA  36b  5k8  7Q2  82T  3T6  4M2  715  784  56o
793  358  5i3  4cn  51a  g61  613  639  q92  25C  4p9  1S8  a37  729  666  6I5  397
Z67  515  F57  5Z7  2j3  836  9lC  5Qs  52V  253  3I5  34p  219  22G  1r8  72u  e39
5sE  94c  843  285  I9E  561  133  834  8Uy  865  7q7  373  2hm  95A  944  261  56H
466  766  96t  1mw  625  812  92o  526  Ix1  f4s  76K  2q8  918  5q5  5O7  266  6AH
V84  546  3u9  7dx  Y54  8e5  I35  87r  168  6P5  148  368  215  6I9  117  7j2  298
V23  81m  23v  m55  83J  n3F  1q4  665  951  589  389  439  Rd4  462  o64  9M6  341
785  46a  211  564  7K2  819  8j7  5k9  211  7KQ  473  448  6wV  2B5  772  7oU  957
1jx  9ha  85z  43k  961  9yH  2I6  q92  553  265  668  948  V61  196  Tw1  R75  232
463  bA2  183  485  2v6  6cE  PF3  8EP  www  395  225  369  885  9O9  367  L66  516
H16  22x  O9O  634  m2S  999  257  255  41b  153  131  225  382  g13  118  238  33F
842  7K8  117  319  k8T  286  413  447  G5i  3g5  812  965  AsF  nM3  776  83G  144
573  gf5  q88  r69  tT1  D61  566  h29  661  472  573  358  224  532  396  6T2  mj5
913  115  991  R23  421  529  8N4  71T  231  K27  2W2  545  rSN  95q  364  341  96V
43m  k2n  972  7Mm  z15  62z  242  132  284  85A  5SQ  777  16D  1vO  69c  98M  4nt
j72  e98  4j9  823  359  483  49z  2RY  2S3  3pZ  Jj9  783  9Cd  4aK  g8V  34r  414
64t  617  711  4h6  pV7  418  248  3w1  51Q  2N6  1J8  55r  963  918  328  2J7  u27
y78  425  819  796  d39  329  6m1  82m  e99  154  P5Y  p33  4o8  n62  j43  V7Z  6S4
```

```
21b Q71 6w8 5oU R1N U94 284 289 215 279 2Y1 222 29P 7I6 162 754 4RJ
3u7 V52 87k 4k1 36e 1Y3 9oL Q5y u59 835 nB9 958 436 3H9 679 455 64A
428 46n JX2 843 WI8 K42 491 529 BE9 1vo 47x 8O5 87P 583 35Z 896 TX8
kk2 E76 7Cb 95n A59 77h 824 645 195 G39 N76 251 353 686 QC7 657 415
183 V38 F63 225 331 3C2 81G 329 32p 538 1M7 3q5 772 bs6 p98 VB9 258
998 P8H 476 776 595 9A1 467 697 T4s 4q5 918 D48 722 334 712 R51 387
89x 6t1 mY1 631 51p 99k w38 2s4 664 K9N 817 675 N92 r85 586 4y5 292
sV3 yXm 3ql 5p2 C7m 83j y1e 775 9e7 288 Q2R oH3 288 476 19C 73k 866
496 1j8 463 4a9 C26 238 818 38m 787 3M2 584 76q Y84 qp3 7I1 toL M41
285 634 3W2 smx X13 eb1 653 955 U95 164 k75 9qS 12E 612 9d4 6R6 0am
2M5 458 451 5T4 YZ1 827 766 849 475 142 562 348 21U y49 368 J76 jFp
855 c11 3ZF 798 483 8w9 9W5 q84 8A5 532 65L 422 56X 781 699 9SS 241
124 448 25x 4Hu 354 521 CI3 kz2 fH1 g1e T29 896 bjG 698 287 VGY 243
R8h 766 911 445 L31 1VN 6U4 925 988 881 815 137 768 666 612 843 596
772 912 2b4 4w6 527 D12 634 559 415 256 228 474 147 821 E42 77o 4QH
f39 752 d3A 675 1z7 6Q7 475 85t 21e B19 519 565 9e3 9LX 5R7 476 88R
6o5 625 36K b5V 734 418 159 9z4 5r8 42N 989 479 574 762 382 863 466
2g3 251 954 x67 9M1 373 G65 351 2A8 O19 268 762 U1A g43 r2V n17 537
13g 945 496 6P4 259 4F7 432 243 57C 461 26e A5l B36 865 x63 622 992
2N5 388 7Ko b93 42s 156 j92 673 8y1 v64 62d Yv6 314 1J4 918 236 713
176 729 966 x58 ea3 vO7 872 231 623 823 424 e44 346 135 1Gm 8gu 537
e7W 1G3 71q DcI 9Q3 953 u57 1t7 717 6kF 2vC M5Y 194 4z4 871 794 PX4
433 785 w82 73g 8b1 97j 3y2 C6U R27 7Mu 219 6n8 8b9 476 2N3 WO5 387
277 4Ag 8F8 14r U5D 8E8 2iy 311 4o9 216 O5Y h31 787 76R 3b1 143 693
516 579 p3K 216 260 652 962 335 464 23w 87j pB6 p85 96z 82W 68P 769
86o 585 917 83L T5j s16 7K2 8M1 386 4VM 684 7n4 2I7 8W5 A81 b53 6B1
u42 3R8 v9E j36 82j 65l 718 78l 365 E25 8z2 62T L34 316 13R 989 xM3
C47 377 872 31O 555 538 688 H63 193 498 p65 438 765 2J4 59a 349 r2U
O1e 8YW 4s5 9E4 UTV 345 839 956 LG6 5QR 1v3 382 x98 s85 9N4 uX5 4YU
594 358 996 222 868 6sM L54 272 RF3 v72 729 9T6 287 6ah 449 824 88a
x59 4A8 o2x 682 P76 68C 866 261 34U 426 k46 869 684 4j7 147 v1G 911
54S U58 31p G67 3o5 667 X31 53N f44 1g6 512 216 164 Z86 137 826 212
498 VG4 713 626 228 38H 51e 93X 445 97U Yj9 19B 984 586 721 TA1 359
994 8E1 429 473 d66 659 148 542 883 1y6 793 w58 345 14t 1K7 66y 7M4
3z1 935 T45 D68 V53 6m9 82Z 569 256 799 39a 9D9 X33 614 741 5M8 K96
J75 N49 g57 561 262 8vt 462 H82 496 775 T39 217 297 k18 586 337 H27
251 385 265 r65 Y68 1F5 593 672 19n 257 5Xs 923 i7O 94o A33 25Q G51
82j t8v 288 F22 dX9 996 2a9 73o X39 158 8d2 664 124 6q6 818 L29 853
4L7 524 4h9 6l6 F77 776 vr7 326 859 68Z 964 281 4Q7 8Ty cQ1 A8S 166
8V2 911 233 141 832 547 99x A59 638 976 T31 2Q8 513 24m 3e3 474 34r
294 G96 129 785 9p7 z61 292 656 C63 Fpf 9T5 c16 bPd 5C6 I25 443 Yn3
838 318 3W8 v7M 61o 971 X28 953 942 R46 1pZ 1I6 s71 42a G24 281 n93
388 836 82W 35r 183 679 314 249 j9h 4P8 262 32M 679 9u4 83U R59 61b
6o4 H1A 5x7 186 246 m2O 9WJ 9Q3 SD8 7CO q37 5P2 39v 197 434 Y83 Df4
w76 Tbq 37p 4ce 835 a35 248 62O I5M 786 452 392 542 46P 688 8w3 386
448 587 99k 37n 567 I74 4Lf 388 969 x33 2L3 X4q 564 477 833 6B8 6q2
77m 976 28g 196 273 7C9 9W5 b32 171 9v5 6m6 V79 2H6 212 821 k98 576
57r z84 x87 775 w9d 837 284 K99 n22 633 94r OpX b98 2D4 881 97W j5M
359 659 957 242 16Z D34 624 7R7 I69 962 hs1 i13 7Y2 e31 61M U1Q gsT
```

```
D25 583 L46 17s 741 972 728 4dl U24 399 586 8SM 93R 847 828 571 9u6
486 K8Y 88z 898 o89 669 72g V92 57Z 35a 4S2 Y33 4U6 63X Q97 RhY 181
474 473 j5k 638 K7U 4i1 692 593 449 132 11c R29 y89 Z55 157 U1E 765
958 411 N56 9z4 V1W 247 521 241 627 941 4z3 N12 Zq9 113 282 13h B35
97P 92b 571 511 85X 98b 745 45i 18g 397 558 1A3 h52 9dC 958 E81 Pr1
766 T79 851 N29 425 745 93F 636 121 51K a54 U61 176 695 X5j 563 c33
345 989 756 664 8Es 77W 86t 7X6 wK6 I81 3WJ O22 B44 1A7 E37 mR1 212
7A4 885 4K1 651 87t 939 6cq 191 759 n2c 845 X14 721 76h 512 861 817
196 423 214 483 15H 942 4H6 x3T N61 7h5 621 474 3r6 359 J94 766 44w
792 56A 7Z7 847 125 I83 598 692 p67 r3D 824 392 76l 432 919 942 566
6P3 n4w 175 32U 678 527 53r 99u 396 Z5Z 124 277 74r 78J 62y 277 5GX
79K 3Y6 U3v Cd9 816 722 9M4 6j8 2O1 4Yi 9v2 466 629 825 3Vk 2iM N36
4w5 J75 566 934 384 258 x72 45D 448 2I8 711 845 L12 83h x8W 181 v22
422 4m7 76Q Q92 96d 6Z4 213 173 519 187 4H4 2rc 121 3H1 364 3T2 369
22N 959 831 994 272 Q32 5s5 w3w 325 5j7 755 125 296 W4v Q5H 95V 5A4
118 694 25J 788 7G6 272 492 258 848 4mb H21 772 9H7 FJO 218 W1s NJ5
876 337 54b 773 414 615 a49 595 756 9r9 7J7 22y 2m7 2u9 122 X78 g92
M7w 5Nj L1N 63i 3c1 886 582 474 14I 82x I47 532 466 793 165 634 3H6
564 9e7 857 769 7B2 6R9 1m2 K39 4x1 455 768 885 345 r63 9c9 Ic4 458
H38 257 673 4v4 A5d 68q 366 199 99z L87 935 767 556 h19 147 317 5T9
f6N 414 524 666 y6B B98 L59 55h 817 2e5 6v5 9v7 G73 976 674 5n4 h29
828 1Z9 558 x56 qe7 287 239 694 4s1 773 5A3 478 952 349 4A1 2F4 747
22e 8M4 Y6i Sp3 72Y S31 957 611 YD6 6FP 1B7 667 q73 j52 B44 57O 5T3
274 775 7y2 77i 216 27z 276 DO6 596 E15 1Y6 419 677 293 U46 4b1 216
T32 14A 537 329 7F6 841 496 73x 596 3I2 915 843 123 981 56G 48U 42j
78L 46u 372 hq6 4M4 638 52u 615 66F 343 e28 76M V89 217 x61 y94 w99
h57 869 241 6j2 733 2Kb 716 483 65V 82b 722 713 553 975 141 363 1B5
9B7 8N5 6W4 43n p77 217 958 152 65L 712 3x9 61l 465 F77 996 298 K65
e68 2MK 858 433 ne3 889 33S 76s 774 684 732 476 a81 mti 946 v23 82r
d93 3w9 596 8U8 zta 86P 4O9 SZ2 2fm 998 77b 615 13x 987 67L L65 936
vR1 p54 634 594 78x pyz 135 Yz9 d7C 8O3 94g 685 26i 664 2T6 179 123
vm9 2P3 217 414 8N1 123 677 7i5 262 757 457 a33 434 171 Ph6 617 h81
3rZ 8r3 4U6 378 249 735 8Mh 353 332 4a7 E2F 1W6 6F8 637 876 s9Q z51
p84 333 256 d22 2v6 7k9 8XQ C28 473 879 6W5 495 643 327 3c6 Q26 283
555 771 122 q49 342 1q5 98s 333 xFe 962 586 694 911 5T6 2S6 3Z4 952
926 794 217 324 691 9zK 699 6g4 5A4 654 8G3 B91 49J 193 A72 894 356
656 GIf 1f7 62M 879 3p4 1g3 6dD OT9 8y2 2w6 14q 679 858 81q 122 8m7
169 72Y Of9 c24 8P9 396 O2h 563 886 4E4 4I6 6BQ 689 Q76 155 71X 957
6B7 755 AkA 829 9x8 751 4Ir 7hK P82 9pw 966 66h a6e 369 468 f44 2J5
745 w18 417 6F4 249 938 731 D78 59b 816 c78 6v1 929 986 783 992 U95
646 eu4 449 m86 996 748 52h 58C 9U3 127 p8w 986 7x8 684 5j8 1V1 1RV
37i 797 474 zi9 2El 248 398 771 348 F31 326 169 S61 iCb 1h3 214 134
k12 98X 377 o35 2I4 oec 233 875 616 U88 6W8 81s 922 154 91C A72 6g1
15o 2a1 5s7 379 315 D28 331 275 961 98l 1R2 79f 5X6 317 169 578 498
12j 6E6 864 e2n 653 7e8 592 w74 4i6 5eq x68 722 S98 878 3d7 899 775
MU1 xUD p29 8y3 743 397 893 15y 48V 595 9Bc 445 2S3 181 77c fvS 756
772 967 253 9K5 575 i53 519 682 616 4fj 3MI 177 8c6 52R 99m N78 697
345 257 9u1 818 968 963 79j 398 4Y8 C87 1F1 7H9 U34 27X 249 B78 2h3
4k7 7mL 968 826 424 881 257 914 914 74r 74e 624 94V 854 67Y 678 548
```

```
5Q9 4B4 8i6 L6u 8E3 5m5 T39 5h9 244 97X 2K5 j1E 615 836 674 966 1M7
AFJ 6G3 184 138 188 k96 861 124 198 19B 63r N5z 92i 723 9T7 3G6 14M
6c8 C25 7Ue 698 e71 Cy8 7Ef x7k 448 k44 Zx6 171 872 534 1u9 551 284
UqA h48 m51 421 W39 9p9 712 H66 174 882 8i3 916 47j 7F2 N4N 26e 6j2
vq1 227 317 825 c78 387 3J4 117 752 1U8 Yz9 755 4m7 995 753 786 5c9
865 198 mW5 98B 774 441 341 389 OT6 524 s21 392 UD8 N89 215 512 K32
qTf y8q 33f 91r EO7 446 3C7 L6U A35 343 3pP T69 7y1 7Yb 92Q 554 3o3
f4c t24 3h1 rT4 287 3o1 V2H 2DG 993 3qW b79 788 52S 95o 281 866 BE3
O36 376 873 1a2 3el 1eN 115 232 a53 262 6K3 54p 751 84c W74 545 7r2
941 12F 3Y1 5JE 819 Q69 j31 996 1k6 198 328 759 198 625 8I2 477 b36
K25 14Y 124 398 R88 b19 853 864 658 158 d67 1sN 37M 3R2 6ob 274 9TH
m74 P93 gt4 572 823 N83 Vz6 857 561 893 517 73P 6W1 25J IaR 78o B83
899 466 324 133 Y51 C6q 97N n2S s62 t45 63h 628 59X 26v 593 126 Yot
G4a 39R 82N 184 V75 379 655 7b5 185 9Z7 887 17s 3C2 2a3 s35 6o3 Do1
739 k7N 4G1 141 96n 961 153 214 9a4 977 727 291 7j9 7l7 417 65R 558
899 Z12 94C 994 P44 154 4E9 9Yy 777 326 96R K19 344 684 198 v2h 29q
NtB 8HX 156 824 306 8BH 2uA 5J9 g11 cy7 217 68v v94 963 47T cz5 757
449 Slg 7K6 6U8 B34 36F 671 59X 8L7 319 2Xa 8X2 U93 6v1 536 355 1w9
5YD WbN k53 225 89K g85 388 571 291 kG3 3X5 731 336 7Ui 253 16r 19u
867 376 97C 919 5I9 271 37Z t45 819 55a i62 78y Da2 56U 1ZT 874 367
698 93Q 8o8 5R1 949 c77 Y3h 83C 452 2C9 68h 575 211 a7Z 785 72I b4R
4gv 19r 151 5C4 427 v89 e4n 45K 763 2iO 178 V91 U75 1a8 9qX y3j 285
w76 98N 9j7 95w 5U2 48T 391 a99 4P4 x5W 96H 84s B24 956 293 1d1 Y36
295 d53 52f 123 581 2Q2 965 778 687 L9h 1XU 952 nW4 C28 3CY 381 13r
238 926 q73 584 Q96 216 8F6 252 6p7 Y6H 953 222 499 1V7 O27 Y54 868
485 236 C88 1j2 678 724 4F6 1s8 n54 88g 42g 432 8Z5 312 992 J81 c34
2A4 b2Z i49 898 854 5u5 84k hqI 81Z d3G 1w5 1e8 2Po 4HY A73 116 543
3vS 41H 694 49Y G56 127 874 259 4w5 752 534 fe3 871 ra9 xZ7 6A5 Q13
434 j92 3W7 3X9 2QM 16e 8Ep 721 k69 f1S g28 7Jr a6a 756 9C8 452 288
73f 832 761 673 6GL 39K 115 311 291 E61 g69 7q9 L65 363 545 P89 699
64f 481 688 266 375 212 9s2 453 826 hf1 266 e82 994 3v5 214 87S a42
381 442 865 6W5 791 1uS Q1B 462 381 721 69E 54e 87H 462 291 T99 956
86w 822 23H 24J 54B D28 2i7 4H6 ZSN 638 538 163 P86 124 922 186 35i
c3o 94k 35v 118 292 dH6 835 U2B 473 U4R 914 h47 d68 4Xr 7Nn 918 232
19p 629 142 988 822 5i8 1n5 915 155 827 mvV 3P9 546 5U8 x81 kN5 761
93q 493 z5c 71z m33 295 2U9 243 859 1cp 937 1dN JS4 657 5u7 864 115
846 5W8 I31 815 49g 385 366 394 725 9U5 4T8 r42 8R3 5t2 e2m N69 c21
42a 4QN e43 421 736 623 5j5 667 63U u65 551 928 59P 1sE 9y6 9Gm 339
416 79l 495 e26 289 h12 5V1 e27 6W2 B8R 859 781 916 938 635 71n 355
433 437 u1h 319 s43 k9T V62 445 wU5 63u 918 479 z33 d77 772 43p 615
B55 81n x46 157 29A 128 hw2 92k cFx 219 132 697 225 A66 315 566 43v
1c7 5P4 222 861 76n 7k5 382 822 927 H2q 4q4 842 S56 813 653 5g5 H1e
5a3 927 976 UF9 639 m64 626 36U 3n7 O53 46R 3x5 f78 93k B1Z 689 t92
V9v 623 73Q 9a7 626 323 7m3 g82 43M V41 KS8 761 z59 53C 4S4 85k 143
1vI 556 5v5 653 917 164 7d7 6go 174 1Go 261 353 2g4 413 42T 33W 886
6i7 y24 788 2E9 8K2 437 436 2a5 621 Opy t4F 287 328 94u 47t 6Y2 Kq2
5S6 278 w14 Z3Q 3S2 248 175 846 567 24N d85 148 661 1L6 813 79U 236
S96 718 352 97s c3F 519 916 1P2 9f1 33h O71 59k 931 3dx 8n5 413 48u
796 926 Pj7 576 21w kK2 6a2 ASQ 355 v69 raZ 3F5 c62 zA5 869 5Hy 454
```

```
464 N6K G85 184 892 387 265 g84 p67 321 879 733 558 pu8 2tP 764 2r4
182 799 O29 37d 468 631 353 94Q u1B 631 877 151 v43 g89 47x 5z9 929
4z1 657 2G6 75r 874 Z56 38l c26 812 822 2g4 51S 961 482 46p 35W 643
q97 618 Y33 148 198 712 9r6 442 41b 549 8rw 4w3 18Y FX9 63z 4M6 693
1o9 jo1 5y9 3n9 558 41Q 172 286 4W4 4iF 9m9 995 486 W83 563 52M 4m5
dt2 525 42r Fsn N6V 797 753 783 7SC 263 5W6 re6 475 86K 9Q3 c72 236
98N 769 7n5 885 332 u25 9o6 6K6 79T 977 53x 5O9 k85 P45 274 Vn9 1E3
2R4 127 674 D81 7S1 MR4 Q3w 2E9 647 313 4Zf 78j 239 hP2 412 2cK 9MC
444 7i1 qe3 826 651 B42 224 877 5P8 612 17h 596 6F3 6uo C98 288 q24
537 6e1 842 37s h22 8M9 21f Y65 272 182 987 979 943 1z1 13o 7o3 I5N
12T 8rV 993 94C 332 415 724 36H q27 858 V5i 863 1F5 633 33v 5j6 422
649 947 155 9FY X77 461 H89 11F 3r1 333 678 626 289 255 2Jx f6S 331
786 14G 753 32a z56 419 348 4Z1 347 465 378 14I q79 J62 562 7p7 dMN
Bw1 72S 963 4i1 976 217 2v3 394 482 fo7 7LM 13f 473 273 T97 376 139
155 449 7F3 2Ab 5Pb 248 1uZ n49 291 V3o 477 541 835 9i4 686 987 s5H
b76 C76 756 Q79 n6J V79 111 24W 17X 771 386 221 67C w7r 5N3 V9o 367
45Y 138 196 685 55f 2i4 Y2F 122 j94 71p 548 596 821 P31 99t Ld1 285
618 22X 991 873 2CU 851 18X 62K 769 3HL 57t 469 357 928 79S 559 sXo
42D 761 177 4S3 733 832 m36 493 j54 174 587 h93 633 97F 4w4 95x b94
385 I57 64T K86 458 442 151 81X W5T 944 t77 577 966 d41 212 865 6m9
795 379 X48 58M 512 4gz 15M f18 C56 9i3 i72 639 632 Y17 gOz 15b 714
385 p3z 29u 61c 308 711 2U2 675 61b 74j w77 4Ut w84 59Z 52j 75K 4N5
I1C 4A2 142 Lbv 424 1Aa G44 578 323 B88 Z37 495 772 2w8 F48 985 9Dc
986 fK4 b9K 19r hW6 u3Y 392 64N 722 8S8 17u 547 115 58t 361 3TO K12
456 579 14c 526 981 778 47n 8P9 553 T27 443 3s2 b39 595 66R 915 231
124 2Wb 956 MvO 1m7 Qd1 oZ8 M44 411 xR8 77v 9D5 98e N23 678 1j4 3jr
154 4y8 u59 835 976 6B8 52c 573 22j 178 174 85P q42 k68 4oJ 77d 143
11K 34Q 63E 8G5 94m 96Z 318 b39 175 3t9 559 336 n98 687 99s U95 B21
7o3 R27 3s8 d84 686 381 827 585 5J8 4l3 378 379 q5E 65p 1Y9 664 t39
2x8 U1w 679 w31 La8 6s5 2C6 72m D67 1H1 237 u54 544 819 322 554 374
lv5 112 2s6 853 64l 944 23e i23 W32 9V9 8P1 848 624 G41 684 tM8 835
cY6 983 192 4zU xn3 67p 116 494 3c7 682 4O9 421 55i 176 8E5 74c 764
r8f 424 6VC 215 578 449 is2 287 2q2 O6K 278 243 12Y 46b 89d G48 2h7
1pM 92s 649 925 84O I34 7O4 737 865 WW7 5s4 33v 895 6w5 334 2MM 916
915 B92 851 161 685 182 384 413 522 299 P84 65r 4i2 Bn3 153 1c6 9e3
48r 6y7 3y4 q1B 723 41w 5e2 564 yO3 9Lm 454 735 211 3X4 938 35M 937
3BB 549 229 78s 878 83N 389 91m w91 934 875 8Q4 438 525 288 995 e14
78z 6L9 949 532 352 945 OJ9 4h5 OF3 56F 9Em 235 V6t 453 4LH 9B7 s3P
Tr7 39W 733 49m 611 L66 16X 43q 22d 2f7 Qr9 M43 25d w35 3V5 X24 p5m
196 311 29f 669 6W8 4n5 2ir 251 6K3 541 533 9h8 386 Y9z 1YM 17j 395
930 534 2n5 676 793 t61 35g 3wO 589 48f 813 H73 8z4 Nj1 759 753 24c
u41 266 425 997 KL8 J47 5nL 129 813 5v5 1J2 428 34i 988 986 Y54 185
X9d VO5 168 1ck 666 691 873 941 8v7 9i5 92i 383 8CY C7W 6m7 K3C 6h2
334 G26 767 435 779 625 824 779 817 1A2 714 5je R61 589 783 T97 Aj8
Q67 297 634 65s 986 96T 3I2 1c2 a3B I72 Vd5 28E B18 O9t W88 K81 73h
52S 191 bi1 663 6aM 414 661 582 139 x33 Lzj 777 218 A5s 656 389 Ke9
p33 45r 35A 169 181 536 981 C12 7h8 47P 78S A8L 97w 2Ud 9B1 5B1 24W
872 169 749 P52 235 817 771 172 vc6 765 96Y 649 EY6 1Z3 11d 132 888
315 844 914 22A 781 293 973 233 144 3iI r24 96r 781 283 1d1 7jC 4WV
```

```
25Z  2D8  927  5N1  858  623  678  22Y  IR7  R69  691  6W8  81i  854  758  56u  25E
931  134  k53  Mj2  1A6  57C  G32  649  lq6  LP4  655  8x4  450  869  175  Y41  844
v67  Ob3  8h7  484  28D  6zc  81g  1Ec  D33  228  x46  q81  Oed  Z2Q  719  7n5  968
55T  K28  428  263  392  666  681  637  8R6  62L  168  651  827  73y  fH3  574  673
4Y7  42p  9h7  148  8m6  9c2  758  4Z9  R6f  835  776  167  5V6  4A1  G15  174  983
389  936  57P  oA6  GW5  618  aO3  r61  232  HL4  5N9  938  9b3  369  3I5  g17  sz9
98X  429  575  6d8  315  sOd  219  722  9zE  883  215  484  Y22  398  DNH  sM2  7Z1
844  245  8Q9  958  262  D46  c36  814  645  977  14m  415  453  844  H45  378  K76
547  h56  478  J62  Z7G  766  241  ny9  662  8W2  464  864  271  475  944  15q  9L9
8D7  363  58J  G55  992  97c  27X  324  637  862  647  s46  384  g77  259  gQ3  r66
662  442  445  4bm  5j5  297  u5j  918  129  485  472  u71  5c3  2K5  69S  378  l38
368  Y25  189  318  512  A78  f23  923  51m  527  1n9  288  536  391  2XQ  T24  78C
64w  482  898  943  69a  Y98  u3S  74Q  8x5  3T1  87n  315  2E3  s8s  554  1X5  9P5
pA2  84y  9tE  34t  1i9  L75  933  ZPE  k48  458  59u  825  831  115  12r  175  233
193  p9m  394  553  7y4  387  649  o32  246  6fG  5w8  854  9yM  4i7  28p  613  658
UY7  963  466  6la  72L  315  351  s65  Aq3  18U  p4t  467  8r1  776  h54  1V5  6pd
47d  1W7  977  82F  514  253  598  k11  I32  971  1KM  9Tm  t41  9b3  2Cj  k77  177
97f  j9d  364  s99  531  Te1  A3g  15p  8cQ  N73  17l  rp6  573  534  Q86  458  6d2
777  VG1  641  G7e  457  558  4P2  6Y7  7c3  5M8  48f  559  N5v  915  K9X  14E  N83
483  345  865  94P  w48  839  48i  3c6  o2f  655  422  526  183  383  J15  225  6W9
4E4  54I  7j2  165  9V5  911  92Q  BO4  841  c91  844  398  V57  952  J92  2J4  41a
726  JN5  837  f21  565  H88  637  467  R73  x18  849  731  Z66  1e2  487  d39  391
16x  13d  S2l  H32  866  7C2  631  FHe  285  688  e81  3W3  D14  984  97z  93D  74k
F96  745  747  627  577  6s8  594  oNC  s1L  71b  hn5  834  542  135  694  717  m65
263  H73  844  o39  689  4C9  r9I  85t  4S7  P59  4e2  44p  7g7  691  7o3  964  232
7r6  412  K5l  e37  686  952  E38  447  k88  B59  21L  K51  85U  1Op  9u5  A53  792
G96  G72  r97  2E5  A29  Dq1  745  3r1  b15  65C  9E2  529  856  L7U  97F  527  4ZZ
R91  121  998  9z6  L91  3j7  971  221  646  798  358  531  929  A17  924  9v2  z64
31t  116  295  957  686  274  G22  625  b69  786  665  tSv  A99  71F  861  v33  525
2U2  823  495  2J6  77g  378  5K5  Z92  141  34P  924  6Z5  A47  655  8C9  24h  988
P41  8Vv  163  754  cWE  59Y  7b4  48z  39L  M72  976  825  uI1  692  22m  45c  81y
46K  3a4  8y9  665  7m1  779  5r4  1wf  1U9  Mg5  97U  548  119  53c  944  467  679
28B  512  9ZM  j2h  3O8  163  414  675  784  h29  35r  357  62M  843  4Gu  3md  682
915  79a  271  k36  y2a  51b  n28  59a  r28  371  22b  277  3u7  854  u58  C71  51t
9B9  H47  538  v9L  A85  972  791  c55  385  N74  618  x63  367  521  82F  54y  13R
7c2  Z75  458  554  2Y1  832  9L4  514  x4t  p44  53S  7ws  p27  711  s57  2R5  584
L43  8E3  M6x  355  N92  V2Z  t69  234  47d  74a  585  16S  3Lk  k94  q73  925  GX6
S2O  551  38X  383  35a  66H  889  AvY  36x  465  885  7n1  51r  971  Kr4  4f6  6p4
937  731  481  628  158  493  h28  U34  277  g67  s43  766  535  85J  172  676  875
58Q  VH5  5B7  689  1u2  P74  233  3qk  25s  649  547  9PY  D83  6J1  8p1  t82  759
328  O88  o78  338  288  696  874  w71  w56  315  195  241  277  M44  318  684  c45
873  693  61r  653  562  58c  288  7j3  478  415  6M2  59i  4M2  9m9  p68  m34  879
75g  u48  K18  432  P3s  795  7O7  736  718  243  k61  995  Co6  4N4  A9K  689  e12
QB3  Ij6  F6A  1kT  877  a44  771  jX9  X88  379  g15  665  95d  612  145  458  555
T15  16j  Hr3  X4f  w4T  91a  X48  63v  6bd  464  41y  993  826  gx6  9cR  17D  354
C5d  dI2  6Tn  591  6E5  894  813  6xu  v3s  879  5e6  5e7  357  6T1  y83  314  L22
532  89Y  163  38P  jI1  831  219  145  955  367  43Q  j11  698  M5U  57X  553  2p6
686  878  46J  194  y7W  425  9b2  795  P1N  I56  hQh  394  217  Z38  169  749  2T5
A6f  892  Y11  782  699  Nw1  627  344  e21  734  76a  7t7  u3z  298  186  M5K  784
```

www.syngress.com

```
759 312 u23 4t5 11x 484 871 291 4g2 9O1 Ae2 FB4 31a 8bY s22 7x8 419
18R XgG 777 732 58F 682 234 N2p 997 M81 642 764 3BA 89r 497 643 s43
A31 719 92W 7Z4 631 513 m5C 779 z84 d61 Y1H 845 361 2HZ l16 F45 174
897 92m Ty8 694 334 866 767 764 Z84 429 836 2J4 59f 69K 396 8A4 46b
325 782 866 D98 563 733 27c 58b 686 Y29 AmT 93g 9v7 T2Q 625 961 B77
595 Lz6 G2B m3f 224 8C9 618 6E1 443 149 621 384 14k zs5 5c7 759 97s
915 916 633 SdD 549 154 Y21 48T 3b2 942 K13 264 F98 5E2 43Q B5y 445
o3u 342 546 t7K 316 471 75O 832 274 455 399 w8e p99 6Tt 193 676 996
771 8f6 437 915 38F o6v 9u6 535 167 59u 343 239 12Q 86X 882 981 850
X23 166 781 54o 5I5 92X 415 498 9N1 11T 297 132 7QV 893 g14 981 4ea
E96 33B z95 61B 3a6 886 924 H15 1o3 285 898 474 q95 j34 95G 618 811
411 9QF 739 Iy2 6gU 139 977 149 877 14E 452 y64 83j 416 682 665 718
112 sJr 46t 9e3 1o6 4Q1 h16 562 62d 1p8 Y55 588 A73 656 9E4 a93 443
r3p 652 tm1 H8S 392 1Z5 qI7 761 a21 324 Ha8 633 426 c65 77v 27p 847
265 167 699 254 17s Q8e 643 724 o65 135 83U 23f K2A p7K 639 U32 955
229 112 4y8 593 453 h2W 962 4g7 8cC 9V1 866 D13 1e4 5D5 132 767 82U
XZ3 199 452 e5V q66 b99 3D3 9jg t12 466 518 295 2S1 52k 42r s71 5F4
j82 11e 877 22n 6R5 448 343 t42 F99 323 9U4 756 252 QHJ 453 256 7qr
18I 3q1 327 q38 543 445 663 D76 251 151 o28 57x 3X2 1m4 39m 2J3 339
476 667 98y 2O6 521 4Q8 474 351 824 G13 321 7t1 312 89m 596 731 317
9Z4 71a 749 25N r4W 1H7 54m 73r 86Z 138 855 49t 58a 342 2me 498 ic4
q5b 239 172 R99 7A5 157 o49 u68 Z6i Tq4 47W 843 1d8 82i 181 61D 436
392 i46 341 1W7 311 739 641 667 7a2 835 717 54I 228 58K 27r e92 679
O43 94v 182 588 5D3 H13 871 1C2 92N S2I 964 K24 812 7Lp 93S 115 O29
878 223 zX6 63G 254 128 63o H98 p55 51J 2U2 4p4 91W 821 36D 73H 5n6
128 3v9 W71 q2x Y62 y42 2e4 999 278 1iX 82Y 94T 528 t2x 412 He4 868
95G 3GL 843 327 3Z7 633 7aQ i7D I35 333 i73 x88 4H2 227 725 17a 274
J26 t19 59Y 614 C22 Q48 mK1 qx4 r11 296 w8X 215 s9Z c17 Z9c L17 17I
E55 241 26h 616 8Vs 414 Y44 63T 732 i69 B15 45i i78 DZ1 938 397 j29
61s 76B 679 74m yS9 Rs3 782 389 Y2P M38 3i3 6O2 1e8 183 36O dmm 136
s6m 4S7 415 27m 48z Q79 559 N39 843 794 813 311 674 363 384 6ZD 76d
298 644 52D H81 A96 64l 7dg 7kX a85 1j5 962 725 z7b J4T 227 712 182
56B I72 2Ty 66p 989 e78 Us2 1g3 1S1 y89 64g 8A2 236 1R5 9O8 191 293
587 128 74s 977 962 s6h 616 O87 31n x12 6A6 778 34I 38K 311 773 767
896 488 137 54q y8M 1I2 79u 722 929 83Q 55Y 47y 452 72e 744 595 311
27T Q26 515 646 e69 t17 44D 7v9 7b4 2g3 4e3 mq2 E28 37i 265 326 197
125 j4H d52 218 S1N 448 191 89f xQ3 9T6 711 56q 3A5 857 33z W49 95i
189 524 467 998 43m 9Y8 246 M23 331 562 A23 129 353 867 O23 1T4 247
888 796 6t5 24Q 5DB 318 h64 246 5Tq T89 z66 82O 9qn 952 Y44 431 293
619 997 b9u 764 456 Eqg 15e I71 487 f93 2F2 15o 1Y8 417 68d K42 12g
731 34E 773 6g9 997 x57 a7V 6N9 2y4 55i G25 165 667 569 119 k86 263
A94 3Y5 584 277 421 931 641 883 51V a87 143 145 8e8 5R5 692 458 512
89v 372 844 3Y2 6M2 4AE 229 366 781 59A Zn2 B66 76a n56 162 9V1 918
99v 342 79t 132 9S3 13o n98 89N 128 581 t91 25m 142 57b 336 153 45V
184 332 662 1Q4 kLd 95L 265 126 254 28H Q39 617 l73 KLa 23T 371 268
NG2 32w 9I9 74i 147 L18 w34 98E 1K9 42K 9jH 21m 561 d1h 183 qj1 136
aG1 889 s6E Tu7 824 25v 4AH Fx9 997 623 3t7 282 8M1 994 799 687 114
81E 4cD 1OB 764 Y53 174 h25 343 191 92L 3f7 N6z 1W2 w86 835 I6r 643
455 553 475 Ue4 362 6FF 3I8 716 136 13H 976 8y7 693 c79 732 tD5 178
```

```
214  FYE  86y  m34  539  46P  h19  353  C66  473  3X3  17k  kN7  22c  cA1  v87  Y51
986  S26  8z5  s5Y  472  296  h54  98v  J57  3X4  96R  w47  R25  471  8E6  9a7  569
866  71Y  Qp7  W45  462  213  63p  437  4c5  285  rF7  46c  826  F35  914  356  Y1B
897  I16  i11  14Y  G34  9P4  82Y  L43  267  K53  832  2k1  995  434  H63  181  746
328  776  573  469  254  897  83c  9r9  76x  9cG  169  u73  831  F5U  9v4  396  6Z7
281  416  83Y  g8D  317  412  2o3  232  Q41  5S8  2oW  133  k82  613  917  616  25q
269  w31  wl5  838  8f1  90s  3vV  4I4  53X  7EY  83e  w23  9r7  336  OU5  549  182
137  i21  612  v9B  Y51  641  55Q  H29  X12  5H5
```

Index

Syngress: *The Definition of a Serious Security Library*

Syn·gress (sin-gres): *noun, sing.* Freedom from risk or danger; safety. See *security*.

AVAILABLE NOW!
ORDER at
www.syngress.com

Securing IM and P2P Applications for the Enterprise

Marcus H. Sachs, Paul Piccard
As an IT Professional, you know that the majority of the workstations on your network now contain IM and P2P applications that you did not select, test, install, or configure. As a result, malicious hackers, as well as virus and worm writers are targeting these inadequately secured applications for attack This book will teach you how to take back control of your workstations and reap the benefits provided by these applications while protecting your network from the inherent dangers.
ISBN: 1-59749-017-2
Price: $49.95 US $69.95 CAN

Software Piracy Exposed

Paul Craig, Ron Honick, Mark Burnett
For every $2 worth of software purchased legally, $1 worth of software is pirated illegally. For the first time ever, the dark underground of how software is stolen and traded over the internet is revealed. The technical detail provided will open the eyes of software users and manufacturers worldwide! This book is a tell-it-like-it-is exposé of how tens of billions of dollars worth of software is stolen every year.
ISBN: 1-93226-698-4
Price: $39.95 US $55.95 CAN

AVAILABLE NOW!
ORDER at
www.syngress.com

solutions@syngress.com

SYNGRESS®